COLLECTOR'S COMPASS™

'50s Decor

Martingale
& COMPANY

Bothell, Washington

Credits

President . . . . Nancy J. Martin
CEO . . . . Daniel J. Martin
Publisher . . . . Jane Hamada
Editorial Director . . . . Mary V. Green
Editorial Project Manager . . . . Tina Cook
Series Editor . . . . Christopher J. Kuppig
Design and Production Manager . . . . Stan Green
Series Designer . . . . Bonnie Mather
Production Designer . . . . Jennifer LaRock Shontz
Series Concept . . . . Michael O. Campbell

Collector's Compass™: '50s Decor
© 2000 by Martingale & Company

Martingale & Company
PO Box 118
Bothell, WA 98041-0118 USA
www.patchwork.com

Printed in Canada
05 04 03 02 01 00   6 5 4 3 2 1

On the cover: *Eero Saarinen Grasshopper chair for Knoll. Courtesy of Standard Home, Seattle, Washington.*

Library of Congress Cataloging-in-Publication Data

Collector's Compass: '50s Decor
　　　p. cm. — (Collector's compass)
　　ISBN 1-56477-346-9
　　　　1. Furniture—United States—History—20th century—Collectors and collecting.
　　　I. Title: fifties decor. II. Series.

NK2408 .A15 2000
749.2'0495—dc21   00-055920

Mission Statement

We are dedicated to providing quality products and service by working
together to inspire creativity and to enrich the lives we touch.

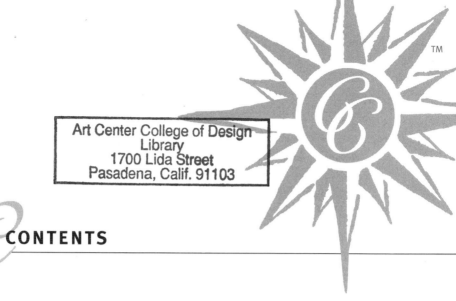

CONTENTS

FOREWORD

As America's favorite hobby, collecting is exciting, gratifying, and above all, fun—but without the right knowledge, you could be destined for disappointment. Luckily, you've just found the most resourceful and inspiring series of guidebooks available to help you learn more about collecting. The Collector's Compass series approaches collecting in a whole new way, making it easy to learn about your favorite collectible categories—from the basics to the best-kept secrets.

The International Society of Appraisers (ISA) is pleased to be associated with the Collector's Compass series. As the ISA celebrates 20 years of professional education and certification of personal property appraisers, who currently specialize in more than 200 areas of expertise, we remain committed to setting the highest standards for our accredited members. The Collector's Compass series of reference books reflects the ISA's dedication to quality and integrity.

Christian Coleman, ISA CAPP, Ret.
Executive Director, International Society of Appraisers

*I*NTRODUCTION

Whether it means setting the alarm clock for Saturday morning yard sales, watching "Antiques Roadshow," or chasing down childhood memories on eBay, collecting has become America's favorite hobby. The joy of finding treasure amid the clutter of a tag sale or a screen full of online offerings is infectious. Who could resist a pastime that combines the fun of shopping, the thrill of the hunt, the lure of a bargain, and the pride of ownership?

Throngs of novice collectors are joining experienced veterans in online bidding and weekend "antiquing" expeditions. If you count yourself among them, this book is for you.

The editors of Collector's Compass realized that today's collectors needed more information than was available, in an accessible and convenient format. Going beyond available price and identification guides, Collector's Compass books introduce the history behind a particular collectible, the fascinating aspects that make it special, and exclusive tips on where and how to search for exciting pieces.

Furthermore, the Collector's Compass series is uniquely reliable. Each volume is created by a carefully chosen team of dealers, appraisers, and other experts. Their collaboration ensures that each title will contain accurate and current information, as well as the secrets they've learned in a lifetime of collecting.

We hope that in the Collector's Compass series we have addressed every area essential to building a collection. Whether you're a newcomer or an experienced collector, we're sure this series will lead you to new treasures. Enjoy the adventure!

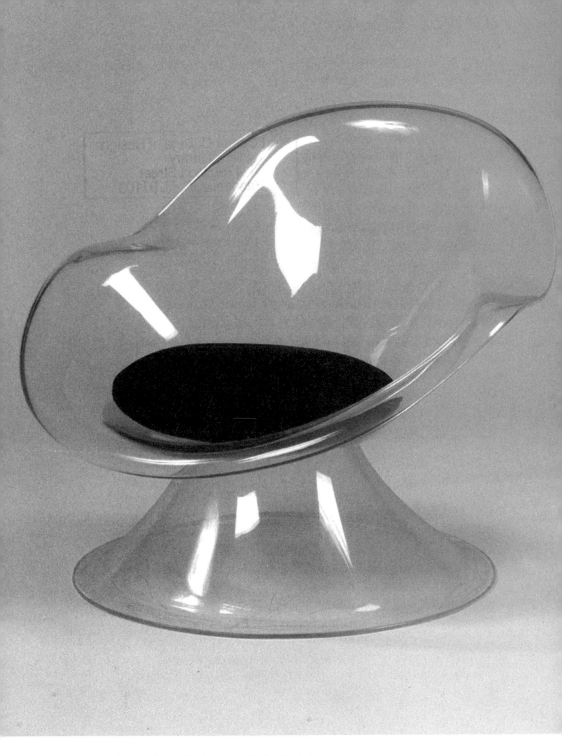

Erwine and Estelle Laverne Daffodil chair for Laverne
Originals, c. 1957. From the 1957 Invisible Group
series, this fluid design predates the popular use of
Lucite in the '60s and '70s. *Photo courtesy of Wright.*

WHY COLLECT '50s DECOR?

The Appeal of '50s Decor

There's a certain amount of nostalgia about collecting '50s decor. Although many collectors did not live through the '50s, there is a sense of remembered time, of a past that seems quite real on one hand and yet distant on the other. Collectors are often drawn to an era that they connect with but didn't live through. It allows a certain romanticism to take hold—of a time imagined but not trapped in the memories of actual events.

Known as Mid-Century Modern to collectors, '50s decor seems to appeal to those who pride themselves on their individuality. Post-war America was a unique time, a time of optimism and confidence, and the exuberance of the designs produced then—from 1947 to 1957—reflect that mood. Furniture manufacturers produced extreme designs—quirky even—that were not marketed as "art furniture" but as well-designed pieces intended to appeal to the public. As it turned out, of course, most were commercial failures. But these groundbreaking American designs with their use of materials such as rubber, molded plywood, epoxy, and fiberglass—some of which were innovations that had helped in America's war effort—made the period a special time. It was the first time in history in which America surpassed Europe as the leader in world design.

There also is a timelessness about Mid-Century Modern. Furniture designs from this era stand out from others; although they may be more than 50 years old, they still feel very modern today. The clean lines and simple appeal of Mid-Century Modern designs are soothing as well as practical; now, as then, they are an antidote to the stresses and "noise" typical of many lifestyles. These were pieces valued as much for their aesthetics as for their functionality.

Best of all, Mid-Century pieces still are widely available on the secondary market, which makes collecting even more exciting. Mid-Century classics routinely show up in garage sales and flea markets, and many great pieces are still in the homes of their original owners. This isn't the case with many earlier collectibles, where fresh examples are scarce and many collections are simply recycled among collectors.

Where to Find Mid-Century Modern

With Mid-Century Modern, as with any collectible, there's always a trade-off between price and quality. In general, items you find at rummage sales and thrift stores will be of lesser quality than those you find at dealer locations. If you enjoy finding bargains, you will need to allocate more time to the search. On the other hand, if you are looking for rare or unusual items, don't waste your time searching thrift stores. Try to imagine where the item you're seeking would end up. If it was widely distributed and was affordable to the general public, it could show up almost anywhere. But if it was a high-end item, it probably sold better in urban environments, and that's where you'll be most likely to find it.

- **Garage sales, rummage sales, and tag sales.** If you're very patient (and don't mind sorting through lots of baby clothes), this is where you'll find the best bargains. Much Mid-Century furniture is still in the homes of the original owners (or those of the children it was passed down to), and some people may not realize the value of the pieces they're selling.
- **Estate sales and auctions.** Many dealers make their living shopping these sales, too, so be prepared for stiff competition. Arrive early and bid quickly; the best items are snatched up.

Estate auctions are your best bet for bargains. Specialty auctions appeal mainly to high-end collectors.

- **Organized flea markets.** These large events attract hundreds of sellers, many of whom will negotiate on price. They're another good source of bargains.
- **General and specialized dealers.** Specialized dealers are great sources for high-end collectibles. But many general antiques dealers also come across Mid-Century pieces and may offer them for sale at below-market prices if they're eager to move them quickly.
- **Antiques and collectibles shows.** This is where you'll see the cream of the crop and learn current market prices. Although prices generally are higher at these shows, the occasional bargain still can be found.
- **Advertisements in trade papers.** Publications such as *Antique Trader* are great places to pick up bargains.
- **Online auctions and live auctions.** Internet auctions on sites such as eBay and amazon.com are increasingly popular (and have generated higher prices due to the wide exposure each item receives). Still, you can find the occasional misidentified or unmarked item at a bargain price if you're willing to devote the time to searching it out.

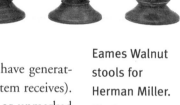

Eames Walnut stools for Herman Miller. *Photo courtesy of Herman Miller, Inc.*

It Should Happen to You . . .

Whenever collectors in any field get together, "fish stories" about incredible bargains and finds abound, and Mid-Century Modern is no exception. One collector tells of a woman in Los Angeles who stopped at a local yard sale and paid a whopping $10 for two Eames child's chairs and three stools. "Together," he figures, "they're probably worth $20,000 to $25,000." He himself once sweated through the bidding at a small auction. He nervously waited to find out whether anyone else noticed that the unassuming little jewelry box that contained a lowly fishing lure also held an Alexander Calder sterling pin. Apparently not. He bought the box for $25 — a few months later, he sold the pin for a cool $12,000.

- **Collector's clubs, societies, and associations.** The acquaintances you make through these associations can lead you to great finds. And if you publish your want list in club publications, you increase your chances of finding your most coveted pieces.

How to Organize Your Collection

A collection without a theme is just a pile of objects. Themes are the links between the individual items—and between the items and us. They tell a story. Whether the story is about the historical time, the designer, or the collector himself, relationships among individual items are what most often give a collection the added character or interest that approaches "greatness." There's no one right way to collect, and creativity is your best ally. Here are some of your options:

- **By designer or artist.** This is the most popular way to approach collecting. Designers and artists were popular for a reason, and there's often more information available about pieces with a specific attribution.
- **By manufacturer.** Many furniture collectors specialize in pieces from Herman Miller or Knoll—companies that produced items from some of the best designers of the period.
- **By pattern.** Collectors of dinnerware often pursue specific patterns. In fact, entire books have been written on this subject.
- **By motif.** Western items, such as cowboy-related decorations and furnishings, are popular Mid-Century collectibles. At the opposite end of the spectrum, so are atomic-era items that make stylistic references to spaceships and satellites.
- **As complete sets.** The mix-and-match approach can yield spectacular displays, but some collectors of bedroom furniture, dining-room furniture, and dinnerware patterns, for example, still like to assemble complete sets of items.
- **By style or origin.** Many collectors prefer a specific style of Modern design, such as Danish Modern. Others prefer the look of furniture from other countries, such as the Mid-Century pieces produced in France and Italy, even though they tend to be more expensive because they were (or have to be) imported.

Whatever theme or themes you choose for your collection, you'll likely want to add pieces on a regular basis. Collecting is an active process—the chase often excites collectors. Learning about Mid-Century Modern pieces, searching them out, and then adding new treasures to your collection are all equal parts of the fun.

A collection also thrives on availability. Many collectors lose interest when their collectible of choice becomes too scarce or too expensive (the two often happen at the same time) or when they've found all the examples that exist. At the other extreme, if items are too readily available, the thrill of hunting them out is diminished, and your collection may become complete sooner than you wanted it to. Then, after all, what's the fun in simply serving as the caretaker of a static group of items? Fortunately, for collectors of Mid-Century Modern, the field is still young; even so-called pioneers with 20 years of collecting expertise are still amassing new treasures.

COLLECTOR'S COMPASS

The Virtual Showroom
Some collectors point to the Internet—and specifically eBay—as having revolutionized the way collectibles are bought and sold. On the Web, collectors now can access merchandise in very specific categories from dealers all across the country or even the world. The only drawbacks: You can't handle the item before you bid on it, and there's often no guarantee. Although the system usually works well, sellers and buyers should take extra precautions with high-end items. E-mail the seller before the auction closes to establish his return policy (if it's not clearly stated in the listing). You also may want to use eBay's escrow feature to help ensure your satisfaction before releasing your payment.

Values and Trends

As a new or aspiring collector of Mid-Century Modern, you no doubt have lots of questions about what you'll find (and who you'll meet) in the marketplace, what you'll pay for pieces for your collection, and perhaps even what your collection may be worth years from now. Although no one can accurately predict the values and trends in any field of collecting, experienced collectors of Mid-Century Modern can offer this advice.

What's the Investment Potential?

New—and seasoned—collectors should always resist the temptation to look at their purchases as investment vehicles. Although it's true that prices for many Mid-Century collectibles have risen dramatically in recent years, the greatest appreciation has occurred only with top-drawer examples that are particularly rare or in pristine condition. Items that are more common have merely kept pace with inflation.

Collectors need to think about the future value of their collection, but they should never lose sight of the most compelling reason to collect in the first place: the love for the collectibles themselves—the subtle (or not so subtle) lift you get from living with them each day. If you build your Mid-Century Modern collection from that passion, you won't be disappointed.

Is This a Good Time to Start Collecting Mid-Century Modern?

Most definitely. Interest in Mid-Century Modern shows no signs of waning. In fact, this young field promises to hold collectors' attention for quite some time as pieces that are still in the homes of original owners enter the market for the first time. Armed with information from books, magazines, the Internet, and specialized auctions, collectors are the ones who ultimately will sort everything out and establish the value of these pieces.

Although Mid-Century Modern is currently in fashion and has been discovered as a hot new field of collecting, remember this: fashion is cyclical. The health of the economy will also affect the demand for Mid-Century items and the prices they bring. Still, in the context of American design, the best examples of Mid-Century Modern will always hold a special place—they'll always be important.

If Mid-Century Is So Popular, Aren't Prices Likely to Be Inflated?

As long as the market continues to get a supply of fresh, new merchandise, prices should remain reasonable. Of course, high-end items in any field will always be in demand and command top dollar. But the vast majority of collectibles from this era sell for less than $5,000—not a low price, but a good value for an original classic design. Down the road, when supply decreases (as it inevitably will), prices will rise accordingly. And that usually dampens the interest of new collectors and the market will likely contract. But the current influx of new collectors turning to Mid-Century Modern indicates that the market is indeed healthy.

Cleaning Up on Clocks

When the price of a collectible becomes exaggerated, it's usually because there are more willing buyers than items available. A good example is George Nelson clocks. Original models that once sold for several hundred dollars now may bring several thousand. Although there's little doubt that they'll always be desirable, some collectors wonder how long that price level can be sustained—especially when dead-ringer reproductions manufactured by the Vitra company are available for about $300.

George Nelson Starburst clock for Howard Miller, 18" diameter. *Photo courtesy of Wright.*

Are There Still Opportunities in Mid-Century Modern to "Buy Low and Sell High"?

You bet. And many dealers prove it on a regular basis when they make buying trips from the East Coast to the West Coast or from the Northeast to the Southeast. They visit a market that may be "soft" on a specific item to do their buying and return to the area where it's "hot" to turn their profit when they resell it there.

But for new collectors whose travel may be more limited, the best way to find the elusive bargain is to know more about a

Florence Knoll settee.
Photo courtesy of Knoll.

piece than the seller knows. In today's market, where information and prices are widely available, finding real bargains is getting harder and harder. But if you're persistent in your research (and your search), you, too, may come across the occasional rare piece that's being offered at an off-the-rack price.

What's the "Typical" Profile of Someone Who Collects Mid-Century Modern?

That's a bit like asking for a description of a "typical" Mid-Century collectible! Collectors range in age from twenty-somethings to seasoned seniors (who may have lived with some of the pieces they collect when they were kids). Mid-Century Modern seems to have a bit more appeal to men than to women, however.

Although there are Mid-Century collectors all over the country (and the world), most collectors seem to be clustered in major metropolitan areas. In particular, New York, Los Angeles, San Francisco, Chicago, Boston, and Miami are hotbeds of Mid-Century Modern. Perhaps not surprisingly, the field appears to attract many collectors who are in the entertainment, design, and fashion industries.

If Mid-Century aficionados share a characteristic, it's probably an eye for the intrinsic design appeal of these pieces—whether it's pure line, novel use of materials, extreme or experimental statement, or even witticism. Mid-Century collectors seem to appreciate risk-taking and a willingness to challenge and even break with convention.

ESSENTIAL BACKGROUND ON MID-CENTURY MODERN

The Origins of Mid-Century Modern

Modern Design was born largely as a reaction to the excesses of the Victorian and Art Nouveau periods. Overly ornate designs characterized these periods, and many people began to tire of them. Modern designs began to appear at the beginning of the 20th century, with European groups such as the Bauhaus in Germany, the Dutch De Stijl group, and the Glasgow School (which included the work of Charles Rennie MacIntosh). In the United States, designers of the Arts and Crafts movement (Stickley, Greene and Greene, and the Roycrofters, among others) proselytized a unified, functional approach to design—from the house itself down to the furnishings, accessories, and decor. Frank Lloyd Wright's emphasis on clean lines and organic designs spawned an offshoot known as the Prairie School. Although these approaches were all somewhat different, collectively they embraced designs that were based more on function than ornamentation.

In the years leading up to World War II, many of the greatest designers of the Modern Movement had begun to immigrate to the United States from Europe. During the 1930s, Mies van der Rohe, Walter Gropius, and Marcel Breuer came to the United

opposite page: Arredoluce floor lamp, 1950s. A classic of Italian design, this multi-colored lamp is made of brass and enameled aluminum. *Photo courtesy of Wright.*

17

States from Germany. The Finnish designer Eliel Saarinen moved to Detroit and helped found the Cranbrook Academy. America's open immigration policy was crucial to the artistic excitement of the era, and in the States, these designers were better able to explore and produce modern designs for a wider audience. Their teachings would influence architects and designers for generations.

With the advent of World War II, production of furniture and the building of new houses came to a virtual standstill. But the war effort spawned the formulation of new materials and methods of production. Fiberglass, plastics, acrylics, foam rubber, and molded plywood now could be used in the manufacture of furniture as well, although it would be several years before that happened. Still, as early as 1940, the potential was evident in the pieces entered in the Museum of Modern Art's Organic Design in Home Furnishings competition. Two men who would in large part help shape the furniture designs of the next decade, Charles Eames and Eero Saarinen, took top honors at the competition. The forms created by these young architects didn't see actual production at the time, but they would influence design for years to come.

After having weathered the Great Depression, the economy was finally being revitalized by the war. Many women were preparing to wed their fiancés returning from the service, and the optimistic years immediately following the end of the war saw a radical change in the landscape of the country. To accommodate all the new families and the corresponding increase in children, housing developments began to spring up in suburban areas all over the

---

Ground Zero of Modern Design: The Cranbrook Academy

One hotbed of Modern Design was the Cranbrook Academy. Located in the suburbs of Detroit, Cranbrook brought together such luminaries as Eero Saarinen, Charles Eames, Harry Bertoia, Florence Knoll, and Ralph Rapson in a challenging environment that championed the interplay of different design disciplines. It was at Cranbrook that Eames met Ray Kaiser, who would become both his wife and creative partner. Students were encouraged to explore sculpting and weaving as much as architecture and furniture design, blurring the distinctions among various lines of study. It's difficult to overstate the impact that Cranbrook alumni have had on the field of Modern Design.

Manufacturers: The Twin Titans

The two most noteworthy manufacturers of the Mid-Century Modern were Herman Miller and Knoll. Both companies still manufacture furniture and furnishings today, although up until recently, they focused on the commercial market.

Herman Miller has been headquartered in Zeeland, Michigan, since its creation in 1923. D. J. DePree founded the company when, along with his father-in-law Herman Miller and others, he purchased the Star Furniture Company. For many years, the Herman Miller Company produced traditional furnishings. But in the early 1930s, DePree saw the need for more modern pieces that better addressed the way people lived. In the 1940s, the company was under the design direction of George Nelson, who recruited Charles Eames and Isamu Noguchi. The designs of Eames in particular continue to define the company to this day.

Knoll was founded in New York City in 1938 by Hans Knoll, who had emigrated from Germany only a year earlier and was familiar with the teachings of the Bauhaus. During World War II, he hired designer Florence Schust, a graduate of the Cranbrook Academy who persuaded Hans to produce her own furniture designs. By 1946, Hans and Florence had married and formed Knoll Associates. One of their beliefs was that designers should be paid royalties for their work, and this ethic, along with their impressive list of colleagues and contacts, led Knoll to hire some of the premier designers of the day. Eero Saarinen, Harry Bertoia, Jens Risom, and Isamu Noguchi were just a few of the names on their impressive roster. In the early 1950s, the company moved from their New York facilities to their now-current home in East Greenville, Pennsylvania.

Herman Miller Home Planning Center in the Carson, Pirie, Scott department store, 1954. *Photo courtesy of Herman Miller, Inc.*

country. A pent-up desire to spend found its way to furniture makers as these newlyweds decorated new homes. And many of these homes were designed with contemporary influences. The modern movement that had never achieved widespread acceptance a decade earlier was rapidly finding an audience.

Suddenly, modern designs were the accepted style. The production methods and new materials made possible by the war meant that more products could be produced at lower cost than ever before. And given the fervent demand for new products, that was a very good thing. What's more, the greater durability of many new materials made these designs especially well suited to the rambunctious families who bought them. There was a willingness among American furniture manufacturers to take chances, and the industry boomed. This was the heyday of Mid-Century Modern.

Countries that Popularized Mid-Century Modern

Where previously, European countries such as Italy and France dominated the market for innovative designs, this period of design was led by the United States. Following World War II, the United States had the resources, the capital, and many of the designers who had fled Europe in the years leading up to the war. That the resulting furniture was being mass-produced largely out of necessity took nothing away from its groundbreaking design.

Charles and Ray Eames molded-plywood pieces: a coffee table, chairs, and screen.
Photo by Charles Eames; courtesy of Herman Miller, Inc.

Although there were some exceptional designs being produced in Europe at the time, they seldom found a market outside their home countries. Today, Mid-Century pieces from European designers such as Serge Mouille, Jean Royere, Marco Zanuso, Carlo Mollino, and Jean Prouve are highly prized but expensive to collect because comparatively few were produced and even fewer were imported to the United States.

Alvar Aalto sofa, model #44, for Artek. The rare sofa version of Aalto's more common chair. Photo courtesy of Wright.

The sole exception was to be found in the Scandinavian countries, where Danish Modern designs became almost as ubiquitous as the Eames chair. In fact, it's still an interesting and relatively inexpensive area in which to collect. Designers such as Hans Wegner, Arne Jacobsen, Alvar Aalto, and Finn Juhl produced some of the most popular and well-crafted designs of the era.

The Philosophy Behind Mid-Century Modern

The goal of Charles and Ray Eames—indeed, of many designers of the time—was simply to offer good design to the masses. The idea that good design could be defined and marketed to the general public was revolutionary at the time, and not all of the resulting designs were successful. For every Eames molded-plywood chair or Bertoia wire chair (accepted mass-produced designs that are still in production today), there was a Marshmallow sofa or an Eames

A 1950s
office setting
featuring Eames
storage units
and chairs.
*Photo by Charles
Eames; courtesy
of Herman
Miller, Inc.*

storage unit—bold design statements that never made strong inroads into the burgeoning American suburbs.

Cost was part of the reason. Designs from Knoll and Herman Miller were never sold as inexpensively as some of the companies' designers had hoped; their expressive use of materials often required extra handwork and expensive tooling. Consequently, many designs sold only to upscale consumers who already had some appreciation of art. It's a bit ironic that Eames storage units, pieces originally intended for offices and dorm rooms, now command as much as $25,000 and are bona fide museum pieces—a far cry from the designers' original goal!

The "Demise" of Mid-Century Modern

Even though it may be convenient to think of the period from 1950 to 1960 as the heyday of Mid-Century Modern, most experts prefer 1947 to 1957. That encompasses the late '40s design icons by Eames and Noguchi as well as the last round of great designs in the late '50s—the Marshmallow sofa, the Coconut chair, and the works of Carlo Mollino and Vladimir Kagan.

Why did the Mid-Century Modern period draw to a close? In some ways, Mid-Century Modern was overtaken by its own success: By the late 1950s, a slew of cheaply made furniture that echoed the curves and forms of the great designs had flooded the market. (Unfortunately, at the time, courts didn't allow patents on furniture designs.) Companies such as Knoll and Herman Miller still produced quality products, but they were often lost in the sea of boomerang-shaped coffee tables and pink Formica. This vulgarization of the classics of the 1950s is what gave the period its unfortunate reputation for producing *kitsch* (or less kindly, junk) and set the stage for design to move elsewhere.

A 1957 George Nelson Coconut chair and ottoman for Herman Miller. *Photo courtesy of Herman Miller, Inc.*

And indeed it did. In the 1960s, Herman Miller introduced a revolutionary approach to office-furniture design (which would later become known as the infamous "cubicle") and dropped many of its classic designs to focus on the more lucrative field of contract furnishings. Charles and Ray Eames largely abandoned furniture design to work on exhibitions and films. Society was losing the innocence that marked the '50s as it prepared for the challenges and extremes of the '60s. And the furniture designs reflected that.

The epicenter of design moved away from America in the 1960s—Britain and Italy defined the look of that decade. But missing in the design world from that point forward was an un-self-consciousness about good design that was a hallmark of Mid-Century Modern. Its best designs never tried to make a fashion statement but were grounded in the belief that good design had something tangible to offer people—something that could make their lives better. After this period, design became self-referential and elitist in ways that great Mid-Century never did.

Back to the Future

No doubt, the close of the 20th century—and the dawn of a new millennium—are in part responsible for the current level of interest in Mid-Century Modern. The year 2000 has long been viewed as a landmark, the gateway to a supposedly futuristic time when we would be living in space and driving cars through the air. Certainly, the designs of the Mid-Century Modern era were more futuristic than those being produced today, so it's not surprising that we're embracing them again.

Materials and Manufacture

Perhaps more than anything else, the materials from which Mid-Century furnishings were made helped shape their form. The materials and manufacturing processes developed during World War II were key to the shapes and forms of the furniture that would be produced over the next decade. For example, Charles and Ray Eames were instrumental in refining the process by which many layers of plywood could be pressed together to create a material of great strength. These molded plywood shapes are a hallmark of the furniture designs the Eameses produced. George Nelson designed a series of Bubble Lamps that were formed by applying a

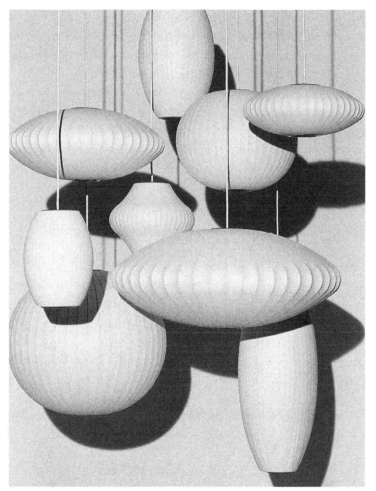

1998 Herman Miller
re-introductions of
the original George
Nelson Bubble
lamps.
*Photo courtesy
of Herman
Miller, Inc.*

self-webbing plastic spray over a metal-cage frame; this spray was originally developed to protect ships in storage after the war. Experimental combinations of materials such as chrome, fiberglass, plastic laminate, and tile were common. And even though not all of these unusual combinations worked, they were a hallmark of the era.

The Importance of Materials to Collectors

The innate durability of the materials used in many Mid-Century designs is somewhat of a double-edged sword. Because the designs *were* so durable, many people used them (and continue to use them), and many pieces available to the collector reflect that wear.

On the other hand, if pristine examples of Mid-Century designs were abundant, the keen collecting interest in them might never have developed. After all, it's the competition for the best examples from the period that makes the pieces collectible.

Some designs were anything but durable, however. The plastic skin of the Bubble lamp is prone to splits and tears. The foam-rubber upholstery of an Egg chair can harden and disintegrate. And any piece with fabric upholstery is subject to wear and fading. It will always be challenging to find these pieces in good condition.

Identifiers and Markings
Common to Mid-Century Modern

There were numerous manufacturers of furnishings from this period, and they all had unique marking methods. Some burnished or branded their marks into the wood—either on the back of the item or somewhere in the interior. Others used various labels or tags, applied with adhesive or tacks, to mark their pieces.

Over the years, these methods and markings changed, and most of these changes aren't yet well documented. For large manufacturers such as Knoll and Herman Miller, more details are known. Especially for designs that have been in production off and on since their introduction, distinct markings can help determine the age of a particular example and will sometimes have a profound effect on its value.

The Packaging of Mid-Century Modern Pieces

Most Mid-Century furniture was purchased off the floor in department stores and boutiques, and it usually didn't come with associated boxes or packaging. Smaller items, such as dinnerware, were usually packaged in plain cardboard boxes, with at most a company logo or subtle design. But because most people threw them away, these dinnerware boxes may add some value to the collectible for some collectors.

Model and Design Codes Used by
Manufacturers of Mid-Century Modern

Some of the best sources for looking up model numbers and product codes are the catalogs produced by furniture manufacturers (or readily available reprints of these catalogs—the originals have become collectibles in their own right). For pottery or dinnerware, original magazine advertisements and illustrated brochures or price lists are your best bet for chronicling the history of a specific pattern or line.

How Mid-Century Modern Became Collectible

The year was 1984, and the publication of a book called *Mid-Century Modern* by Cara Greenberg is credited by some experts as signaling the beginning of the field as a collectible. At the time, most Mid-Century Modern collecting centered in New York, Chicago, Los Angeles, and San Francisco. Pioneer collectors such as David Salle and Robert Mapplethorpe were making a name for themselves. When the influential gallery Fifty-50 opened in New York City in the early 1980s, prices for Mid-Century pieces were only about 10 to 25 percent of what they would be by the end of the century.

The Early Appeal of Mid-Century Modern

Against the backdrop of the stripped-down black designs of the 1980s, Mid-Century Modern was primed to be rediscovered. Then, as now, the obvious power and beauty of the best designs spoke to early collectors. Although some of those pioneers like to refer to these as "the good old days," when prices were a fraction of what they are today, it wasn't always easy to identify the truly noteworthy or rare designs when the field was so young. Today's collectors have the advantage of a much broader knowledge base, and they're taking advantage of it to discover exciting new treasures.

Noteworthy Collections of Mid-Century Modern

No doubt, there are many exemplary private collections of Mid-Century Modern being built right now that will later join this list. But for the time being, here is a short sampling of stellar collections from around the world:

- The Eames Office Gallery and Store in Santa Monica, California, features rotating exhibitions from the Eames collections.
- The Vitra Museum of Germany owns the premier collection of Eames design.

- The Knoll Museum located at company headquarters in East Greenville, Pennsylvania, has built a collection of more than 90 objects no longer in production.
- Most museums that house modern art also are beginning to acquire collections that include Mid-Century designs—notably the Museum of Modern Art and the Cooper-Hewitt National Museum of Design in New York, the Philadelphia Museum of Art, and the Montreal Museum of Decorative Arts.
- A well-known early collection by Michael and Gabriella Boyd has been the subject of a book and museum show.

Organizations for Collectors of Mid-Century Modern

Most formal collectors' clubs are narrowly organized around specific collectibles such as pottery, ceramics, or even a specific dinnerware pattern. A few have formed Web rings on the Internet to keep subscribers informed and to foster conversation among participants. These groups operate via e-mail, so keeping up with them is as simple as reading your daily e-mail and responding when you feel like it.

The Best Sources for a Quick Education

Magazines

- *Echoes,* in which decorating is a focus, can often be found in 20th-century design stores or specialty magazine shops in urban areas. It is also available by subscription. It features listings of shops, Web sites, resources, informative articles, and interiors filled with Mid-Century decor pieces.
- *Modernism* is published by auctioneer David Rago and edited by Cara Greenberg, author of the seminal book *Mid-Century Modern.* The emphasis here is on information rather than decorating.

Books

- *Contemporary* by Lesley Jackson. The original hardback edition is sometimes difficult to obtain, but the softcover edition is readily available. This is a wonderfully illustrated book with more information about architecture and style than individual furniture pieces.

- *Mid-Century Modern* by Cara Greenberg. The original hardback is out of print and sells for $100–$150 on the secondary market. The softcover edition is still in print, however, and contains the same information but includes an updated listing of resources.
- *1,000 Chairs* by Charlotte Fiell and Peter Fiell. This book provides a good overview of most of the great chair designs of the period and also features modern chairs of other collectible periods and mini-biographies of many of the century's greatest designers.

Web Sites

- **Deco-Echoes,** www.deco-echoes.com. This Web site is sponsored by the same people who publish *Echoes* magazine. It features a directory of shops and links to other 20th-century design sites.
- **Design Addict,** www.designaddict.com. This Belgian Web site (written in English) features helpful links, classified ads, and a message board.
- **GoMod,** www.gomod.com. This Web site is one of the only portals to other Mid-Century Modern dealers and resources, and also features information about scheduled events, facts on the history of the collectible, classified ads, discussion groups, and scheduled chats.
- **Herman Miller,** www.hermanmiller.com
- **Knoll,** www.knoll.com

Other Sources

- **Auction catalogs.** These resources are invaluable because they help set the market prices of Mid-Century Modern pieces. All are available by subscription or single copy. Back copies are available from The Catalog Kid at www.catalogkid.com. Treadway Gallery Auctions, David Rago Auctions, Los Angeles Modern Auctions, Wright Auctions, Sotheby's, and Christie's are the most well known. Be aware that all except Los Angeles Modern Auctions also deal in other periods, so be sure to request subscriptions or copies specifically for 20th-century design.

BEFORE YOU START COLLECTING

What You Need to Know About the Marketplace

As you're about to see, there's no single "marketplace" for Mid-Century Modern. Rather, the collective marketplace consists of everything from the garage sale down the street to a variety of dealer locations to high-end auctions at well-known houses such as Christie's and Sotheby's. And for the new collector, each marketplace sector offers its own special opportunities and has its own set of rules. Here are tips on some of the most common. Because dealers and auctions (both live and online) are so important to Mid-Century collectors, they'll be covered in greater depth later.

Garage Sales, Yard Sales, and Tag Sales

These venues definitely are entry-level picking, and there's a certain amount of luck involved in coming away with great finds. But when you're lucky, you'll almost certainly get a bargain price to boot. Your best bet is to target older neighborhoods. Scour the newspaper the night before and plan your route. And plan to start early: For sales that start at, say, 7:00 A.M., the best items will almost surely be gone by 10:00.

opposite: Mid-Century Modern pieces rise high in Standard Home, a specialty shop in Seattle.

COLLECTOR'S COMPASS

The Golden Rules of Collecting

1. Buy Quality, Not Quantity.
It's all too easy to buy many items of inconsequential value—and to spend a fortune doing so. Try to buy the very best you can afford of whatever it is you like to collect.

2. At the Beginning, Spend as Much on Books and Subscriptions as You Do on Collectibles Themselves. Not every item you'll come across will have collectible value. A little education will go a long way toward giving you the correct vision of what's truly valuable.

3. Collect What You Like.
No one can predict which items will increase in value. So it's important to enjoy the pieces you buy for what they are, not as potential investments.

4. Be Active.
Networking with shop owners and fellow collectors is one of your best collecting strategies. It's important to continue growing in your knowledge about the collectible and to gather firsthand experiences at a variety of outlets.

5. Be Patient.
After you've been collecting for a while, you'll come to realize that more good items come along than most of us could ever hope to afford or even accommodate in our homes. Try to focus on the pieces you truly value or that have a great value themselves.

6. Be Fair.
Take pride in conducting yourself in a respectful and generous manner. Building relationships is the key to building a great collection, and collectors reap what they sow. In the long run, your fairness and generosity to others will come back to you many times over.

7. Add to the History.
Keep good records of the items you buy. Remember that you're a link in the story each piece has to tell. Try to leave your pieces in the same—or better—condition than when you bought them.

8. Nurture Your Personal Vision.
Don't let reference books dictate what you should and shouldn't collect. "Collecting by rote" is a lifeless pursuit. Look beyond the icons in the field, and let your creativity and personality guide your choices.

Estate Sales and Estate Auctions

These are great places to find Mid-Century pieces, but competition is fierce and you'll likely see dealers from shops you frequent in line ahead of you. Estate sales operate in different ways, but generally they'll hand out numbers to those arriving first. At a usually preset time, they'll open the doors to those with the lowest numbers. Expect to get up early and to write off any other sale venues for the day. But if you happen to pick the right sale, these sacrifices could be well worth it.

Prices are usually a bit higher than at yard or garage sales. And because these sales frequently occur after someone's death or a move to a retirement facility, estate liquidators often administer them. In many instances, these liquidators already will have cleared out the best items (in their opinion) for their own auctions or shops. But the good news is that their opinions are often wrong! Still, be prepared to act quickly. The best items go fast.

When the Early Bird Doesn't Get the Worm

When you see a "No early birds" notation in classified ads for sales, please take it to heart. Preparing for a garage sale or yard sale is a time-consuming chore that involves staying up late the night before and getting up early the day of the sale. If the sale notice specifies a start time, don't arrive an hour earlier—or worse, the night before—hoping to cherry-pick the best pieces.

Estate auctions give you a bit more time to consider your purchases. Use the time well, because purchases here are usually final. Decide in advance what you think an item is worth and the top price you'll pay for it, and bid accordingly. And be on the lookout for fakes or misrepresented pieces—unscrupulous sellers often plant them at estate auctions.

Flea Markets, Bazaars, and Thrift Shops

Some Mid-Century collectors insist that these are their favorite places to shop. They're a nice middle ground, they say—they yield more finds than days spent at garage sales but lower prices than specialty retail shops.

The quality of flea markets and bazaars varies widely, however. Focus on those that sell collectible merchandise—not new items. Thrift shops, on the other hand, can be hit or miss. They're known for marking items at below-market prices (for fast inventory turnover), but the individuals who operate them often have little knowledge of specific fields of collecting. On days when new shipments arrive, some collectors visit their favorite thrift shops two or three times to get first pickings.

Consignment Shops

Consignment shops offer merchandise for sale at a fixed price, of which the owner keeps a small percentage. This lets the shop owner (the *consignee*) create an inventory at little or no cost and gives the seller (the *consignor*) the advantage of receiving potentially more than he or she would get selling outright to a dealer.

When you buy from a consignment shop, it's important to realize that the shop owner may receive only 10 to 30 percent profit from the sale (compared to 50 percent profit for specialty retail shops). Most consignment shops discount at fixed percentages on a fixed schedule. In other words, if an item goes unsold for a specific period of time, the price will be discounted. If it sits unsold for the next period, it will be further discounted, and so on, until sold or withdrawn by the consignor. It doesn't hurt, however, to ask for a discount if you're not willing to pay the price marked; sometimes the dealer will call the item's owner to see if your offer affords both consignor and consignee sufficient profit to be acceptable.

The Internet

Thanks to Internet sites such as eBay and amazon.com—as well as proprietary sites operated by specialty dealers—Mid-Century Modern has reached the masses!

When you buy over the Internet, consider the reputation of the seller. Have they been in business for a relatively long time or just a short while? Do you know anyone who's had experience with this particular shop or dealer? Although the vast majority of sellers on the Internet are fair (especially so in the field of Mid-Century Modern), it still pays to be cautious with big-ticket items. EBay's feedback feature is a good indicator of a seller's reliability; an unblemished record of positive feedback gives you some assurance that you're dealing with someone who's reputable and will stand behind his merchandise.

In most instances, you'll pay the shipping costs to receive your treasure and, in the case of furniture, this can be more than just a nominal expense. In the off chance that you're not satisfied with your purchase, you probably can return it—but at your expense. A few well-chosen questions about the condition of the item may prevent this scenario. Also, reputable dealers will accurately describe the condition of their items in the first place.

Antiques and Collectibles Malls

Much as the Internet has exploded in recent years, antiques malls have undergone a similar explosion in the last decade. Although in major cities there may be malls that specialize in Mid-Century, general antiques malls usually aren't the best places to find quality pieces.

Malls generally allow a set discount—usually 10 percent—off tagged prices. If you find a piece you like, by all means, ask for a discount off the listed price (or for more expensive items, make an offer). In either case, the mall may have to call the owner of the item, and some of them will not be willing to do this.

The main drawback to buying at malls is that, in most cases, you don't have contact with the actual seller. You get no information about the history of the piece, and there's no opportunity to build a dealer relationship. You have to make a buying decision based on the piece that's in front of you, and there's rarely a guarantee.

Specialty Shops

Individual dealers are a great source of Mid-Century Modern—especially high-end items—and they're no longer confined just to New York, Chicago, Los Angeles, and San Francisco. Find shops near you through advertisements in *Echoes* magazine, *Modernism* magazine, and Internet Web sites such as deco-echoes.com and gomod.com. Also check your local Yellow Pages under "Antiques." Whenever you contact a new dealer, ask for referrals to others who also might offer items you're looking for.

Specialized dealers often sell the best examples (and usually with a guarantee), but they sometimes charge much more than you'd pay for a similar item at a flea market or antiques mall. That's their biggest drawback.

Antiques and Collectibles Shows

Don't underestimate the importance of specialty shows. The best ones give a cross-section of the market—and they're a great way to meet the major dealers in person.

Plan to be at the show when it opens. That's when the best items are sold. Beforehand, ask the promoter for a layout of the show and a dealer listing. Go first to the booths of dealers you know and with whom you've had good buying experiences. Then shop the rest of the show in a systematic manner.

On your first pass, concentrate on the booths at the back of the venue, where the rents are probably the cheapest. Rare items usually don't last long there. Then move to the front, shopping at a normal pace but not taking time to chat (tell friends you'll come back later). Take a short break, and then go through the show again, this time talking with dealers and asking questions about specific pieces. Take notes. What was the best item you saw? What was the price? If you're still shopping at the end of the show, this can be a great time to find bargains—many dealers would rather sell a piece than pack it up and cart it home.

Join the Mid-Century Collectors' Community

Before the Internet, there were few opportunities for Mid-Century collectors to exchange information with each other. But now there are numerous Web sites and Web rings devoted exclusively (or in part) to Mid-Century Modern, many of which offer community areas where visitors can share information. In essence, these message boards and discussion groups serve the same purpose as the collector's clubs of the past—but with the added advantage of unlimited geographic boundaries.

On the Internet, visitors share tips on their favorite sources and shops, the care and restoration of their prized pieces, and dates of upcoming sales and events. This also is where some members first publicize pieces they're offering for sale—giving regular participants the first opportunity to buy items that may be highly prized collectibles.

Dealing with Dealers

As a new collector, you'll soon discover that dealers are just about everywhere. They're the people selling to you at flea markets and specialty shops. And they're also likely some of the competitors trying to outbid you on the items you want at auctions. Dealers are such an important source for collectors—for valuable information as well as collectible pieces themselves—that it pays to know the ins and outs of working with them. Cultivating relationships with your dealer network will pay big dividends in building a quality collection.

Can I Rely on Dealers to Know
Everything There Is to Know About
What They're Selling and What It's Worth?

No dealer can be expected to know everything about everything. In fact, it's good that they don't—the occasional times when you happen to know more about an item than the dealer who's selling it are when you'll snag real bargains.

Dealer knowledge varies widely. Savvy collectors ask their dealers questions—lots of them. Specifically, ask why the item is priced as it is. The dealer may be willing to give you some sort of context for the asking price. By questioning pricing, you may subtly get the dealer to open the door for negotiation. Dealers generally try to acquire items at about 50 percent of the price they believe to be the current market value, giving them 100 percent mark-up. They may acquire a highly desirable piece for more than 50 percent of its value because they expect to trun it quickly and it adds luster to their inventory.

That said, it rarely pays to call attention to a dealer's error—even when you know you're right. Always remain polite and nonargumentative. Listen to everything the dealer says, and then evaluate the truth and logic of what you hear.

Are Most Dealers Honest?

Fortunately, yes. Dealers who habitually lie to their customers don't stay in business long. But that doesn't let you off the hook for doing your homework and asking lots of questions. Dealers aren't out to cheat people, but they aren't always as careful as they might be, either. For example, even though the dealer believed in a piece enough to have purchased it himself, it's possible that he overlooked something or just made a mistake.

COLLECTOR'S COMPASS ™

Want-List Wonders

Creating a want list of the specific pieces you're looking for is a great way to get dealers to remember you and call you. An up-to-date want list in the hands of a dealer who knows you is one of your best guarantees of finding the pieces you truly want. Leaving a want list in no way obligates you to buy a particular item, but before you print out your list and cast it to the four winds, take a moment to consider the price structure of the items you've put on it.

For example, if you've listed a Marshmallow sofa, but you're only willing to pay less than $10,000 for it, most dealers won't take you seriously. To make the most of your dealer network, you should be willing to pay somewhere within the range of the typical market prices for the items on your want list. This doesn't necessarily mean top dollar, but you'll find that dealers seldom call collectors who are looking only for "wholesale-price steals" on their want-list items.

As a new collector, you'll rarely go wrong if you stick with dealers who've built solid reputations. Ask around. And never enter into any major purchase without some sort of written guarantee that also notes all pertinent facts about the item. A dealer who's unwilling to accommodate you on this doesn't deserve your business.

How Can Dealers Help Me Build My Collection?

Probably in more ways than you can imagine. First, most dealers love to talk about their merchandise and in so doing, will give you invaluable insights and information. After all, part of their job is educating buyers about the field they love.

Second, by building a long-term relationship with a dealer you like—by being an active collector who makes regular purchases from the dealer—you'll earn a spot on the dealer's A-list. You'll be among the first to receive a call when truly special items appear on the market. And often dealers will underprice their best things, making these rarities well worth snatching up.

I've Heard that Some Collectors Buy Pieces from Dealers "On Approval." What Does That Mean?

Glad you asked. That's yet another way dealers can help you fine-tune your collection.

After you've established a solid relationship with a particular dealer, it's not uncommon for the dealer to let you take home a piece you're especially interested in to see if it really works in the context of your collection. Typically, you and the dealer will work out the price and terms of payment in advance; please don't commit the faux pas of asking the dealer to negotiate on price after you've already taken delivery of the item and decided you want to keep it. Also, don't expect dealers to extend this courtesy at shows. Shows are limited-time selling events, and most dealers can't afford to remove an item from display, even for a short time.

Are Dealers' Prices Ever Negotiable?
Certainly. Never be afraid to bargain—it's part of the fun of collecting. In fact, most dealers factor in a certain amount of "wiggle room" in their asking price—anywhere from 10 to 20 percent.

Just be sure to keep your negotiations positive. Refrain from nagging, pointing out flaws, or otherwise insulting the merchandise. If a piece seems expensive, ask the dealer how he arrived at the price. You might say something like, "I really like this piece, but I can't pay what you're asking for it." Or you could take an even more direct approach and simply ask, "Would you be open to an offer on this piece?" Take your

> ### *"I'll Take It!"*
> A word to the wise: On those supremely memorable occasions when you happen across a sought-after item that's ridiculously underpriced, simply say, "I'll take it!"
>
> Don't discuss. Don't negotiate. Just buy it and walk away. The dealer will almost certainly eventually realize his mistake. And although it's fair to buy a bargain, don't add insult to injury by asking for an "additional" discount.

time. The more time you invest in your discussion with the dealer, the better your chances of getting the piece at close to your target price. But a word of caution: If you and the dealer reach common ground in your price negotiations, by all means, be prepared to buy. To a dealer, there are few things worse than customers who negotiate as a game and really have no intention of buying.

Is It a Good Idea to Leave a "Standing Bid"
with a Dealer for a Particular Piece?
A standing bid—the top-dollar price you're willing to pay for a piece—could end up working against you. That's because dealers can use it to "shop the piece around" for slightly more money. And

why not? Another potential buyer might easily conclude that if someone else is willing to buy the piece at this price, it must be worth it.

Your offer will be more compelling when there's some immediacy to it: Say, "I'll buy this piece right now for this price." Of course, that doesn't mean you wouldn't also buy it later for the same price, but such a statement might prompt the dealer to act. If the dealer asks whether you'd agree to that price at some future time, simply say, "Perhaps, if I haven't bought anything else by then." Most dealers will realize that a bird in the hand is worth two in the bush!

Should I Request a Receipt for Every Purchase?
Yes, definitely. And it's best if the receipt includes the dealer's name and address, your name, and a description of the piece you've bought (including its approximate age and its condition). The sole exceptions: garage sales and flea markets, where some vendors won't give receipts. At these venues, simply record the details of your purchase in a notebook.

Finally, don't be put off if your receipt includes an added amount for sales tax. Full-time dealers are required to include it, and increasingly, state agencies are monitoring their compliance.

What Is My Recourse If
I'm Not Satisfied with My Purchase?
Most dealers will gladly give you a refund if you promptly return the merchandise in the same condition. But you should always ask about a dealer's return policy, and once again, getting a receipt that describes the item is your first line of defense. Then, if you later discover that the piece isn't authentic, you've got something in writing to back up your claim. Whenever you buy a high-ticket item, you should ask for a written guarantee as additional protection. Condition is another matter, however. Carefully inspect the piece before you agree to buy it, and specifically ask the dealer questions about its condition, the originality of all pieces, and any history of repair, refinishing, or restoration.

Participating in Auctions

Online Auctions

Where Can I Find Online Auctions?

eBay is arguably the most popular auction site on the Internet. When you call up the eBay home page at www.ebay.com, you'll see that the site is organized by items of interest. Whether you're a buyer or a seller, there are appropriate buttons to click for help and additional information.

Amazon.com and Yahoo Auctions also operate auction sites that sometimes feature Mid-Century collectibles. By visiting a popular search engine such as Yahoo.com and entering "online auctions" as your search term, you'll generate a long list of other sites to check out, too.

How Do I Register for an Online Auction?

On eBay, one of the first things you'll see on the home page is a "New User" section. This explains the details of bidding and selling on eBay, both of which require you to register. To register, you must have an e-mail address. You then access the registration page on the auction you're interested in and enter personal information such as your name, address, and e-mail address. The eBay registration page can be found at: http://pages.ebay.com/services/registration/register.html.

To sell items, you'll have to place a credit card number on file. There's usually a small fee charged for placing an item on auction and then a commission charged when the item is sold. These charges are made directly to your credit card account. You'll receive a monthly statement of charges to your credit card from the online auction.

How Do I Search Out the Items I'm Interested In?

Try searching under the name of the designer or manufacturer, such as "Eames" or "Knoll." Keep in mind that most other collectors will be using the same terms to find items, so these auctions tend to be very competitive. The savvy searcher will come up with less obvious terms that may produce misnamed or unmarked items. Perhaps by searching for "plywood chair" or "modern sofa," you'll come across the same items at lower final bid prices.

What's the Best Strategy for Bidding in an Online Auction?

Although some bidders like to open with the highest price they're willing to pay at the start of an auction (to discourage others from bidding), most bidders prefer to wait until the last possible moment before the auction's close to place their bid. That's because all bidders enter their user name, and other bidders can use the search engine to see what other items a particular bidder may be interested in. That way, they often come across items they otherwise might not have found. By waiting until the last moment to bid, you can minimize this method of discovery.

Known as *sniping,* this practice of waiting until the last moment to bid is considered unfair by some because it may not allow an item to reach its true price potential. But whether you place your maximum bid early or at the last minute, if there are multiple bidders for an item, the highest maximum bid will top all others by the auction's standard increment, even if this occurs in the final seconds of the auction's close. The only difference is that the bidding takes place at the speed of light—faster than any human auctioneer could call the bids! Many new auctions prevent sniping altogether by extending the auction deadline for a specific length of time if a bid comes in at the last minute.

What Are Seller Reserve Prices?

The reserve price is the lowest price that the seller is willing to accept for an item. This amount isn't disclosed until the close of the auction. If the item reaches its reserve price, the auction will indicate that the "reserve is met" and the item will be sold.

How Does the Transaction Take Place If I Make a Winning Bid?

If you've placed the winning bid on an item, you'll see your user name listed as the winning bidder on the item's auction page. The auction then will notify both you and the seller and provide your respective e-mail addresses. The seller will send the successful bidder a note of congratulations and explain shipping and payment options. Once you've made payment and received the item, it's customary to notify the seller that it was received in good condition.

What If the Item Arrives and It Wasn't as Described?
In that case, the seller should let you return it and refund your money. But if the item was correctly described and you're simply unhappy with it, you're probably stuck with it.

When the transaction is complete, each party should "post feedback" into the other party's profile. For example, if you made prompt payment and conducted yourself in a businesslike manner, the seller should give you positive feedback. If the seller shipped the item promptly, packaged it sufficiently, and worked to resolve any disputes, then it's customary to give the seller positive feedback. Negative feedback usually is a last-resort measure reserved for instances in which all methods to resolve a dispute have been tried but to no avail.

What Are the Pros and Cons
of Buying in an Online Auction?
Online auctions have provided greater access to collectibles than has ever existed. They've leveled the playing field, giving people in all areas of the country—and around the world—equal opportunity to sell and bid on items.

Still, some collectors are justifiably nervous about the unsecured nature of online auction transactions. It requires trust to bid on an item solely on the basis of a digital photo and a text description. Payment must be sent to a stranger before the item is even shipped, and if you're unhappy with it, you may have limited recourse.

Still, the vast majority of these transactions turn out well for both buyer and seller. If you're still unsure about bidding—especially on a high-ticket item—don't hesitate to inquire further about the item's condition or even request additional photos. And it never hurts to ask for a guarantee that you'll be able to return the piece for a refund if it's not in the condition advertised.

Live Auctions
How Do I Find Out About Live Auctions?
Live auctions—auctions that take place before a live audience—range from local countryside events attended primarily by friends and neighbors to large auctions in urban centers where museums,

collectors, and interested parties from around the world may converge. *Echoes* magazine and *Modernism* magazine publish notices of auctions of interest to collectors of Mid-Century Modern. Local newspapers also list auctions in their classifieds sections, but it may not always be easy to tell if they'll include Mid-Century pieces.

What's the Role of the Auctioneer and His Crew?

The auctioneer takes bids for the items. He or she will pick up or point to the item up for bid and briefly describe it. Auctioneers are usually paid a commission based on the final selling price, so it's to their advantage to get the highest possible price for the items. It's the job of the crew to take the items to the auctioneer and to remove them once the bidding is over.

How Should I Prepare for a Live Auction?

If at all possible, inspect any items you're interested in firsthand before the auction begins. Many auctions post scheduled preview periods, sometimes the day before or early on the morning of the auction. This is especially crucial for expensive or rare pieces and at smaller auctions that don't guarantee sales. If you can't look at an item in person, request a detailed written condition report for it.

Next, decide beforehand what you're willing to bid. This will help you avoid being carried away by a frenzied bidding war and paying more than the item's true market value. In arriving at the maximum price you'll pay, be sure to factor in any buyer's premiums that may apply. Essentially a practice of "double dipping," buyer's premiums are commissions the auctioneer charges to the winning bidders (in addition to the commission he receives from the items' owners). Be sure to determine if a buyer's commission will be charged when you register to bid. Also figure in the cost of shipping, if applicable, when you calculate your top bid.

Is It Difficult to Register to Bid at a Live Auction?

Not at all. You can probably even do it by mail. If you have a driver's license and a credit card, you're all set. Some auctions also ask for credit references and a bank reference if you plan to pay by check. You'll be assigned a bidder number, and at the more established auctions you'll be issued a paddle showing your number.

Exactly How Does the Bidding Work at a Live Auction?
As in online auctions, some items may have reserve prices. The auctioneer will determine the opening bid based on this reserve and on any absentee bids received before the sale. Often, bidding will start at about half of the item's "low estimate." For example, if it's expected to sell for between $600 and $1,000, the auctioneer may start the bidding at around $300.

Then as bids come in, the bid price will be escalated in a tiered manner—usually in increments based on the dollar amount of the bid. For instance, between $100 and $500, the bid may increase in increments of $10; when the bidding reaches $500, it may increase in increments of $25. Once the bidding has topped out and the auctioneer receives no further bids, he'll close the bidding, usually with the stereotypical "Fair warning, going once, going twice, sold." If you happen to be the successful bidder, you show your paddle or call out your bid number. In the event that the bidding never reaches the reserve price, the auctioneer simply pulls the item, and it's not sold.

What Price Paper?

So what if you don't set yourself a bid maximum for an item on auction. What's the worst that could happen? Well, consider the poor (now literally) collector who sent a dealer to an auction with the assignment to win him a rare original catalog by a noted designer. The dealer promptly got into a bidding war with another collector and bought the paper catalog for the stunning sum of $17,000—easily ten times what it was reasonably worth.

Experienced collectors will tell you to avoid making the first bid. But once bidding is underway, make sure the auctioneer can see you. Don't hold off bidding until near the end (this isn't an online auction, after all) or otherwise try to "time" your bids. Just speak clearly, make eye contact with the auctioneer, bid until you're done, and then stop. Good luck!

Can I Still Bid on Items If
I Can't Be Present at the Auction?
Yes, indeed. Of course it's always best to bid in person. But if you can't be present, you can preregister and submit bids for all items you're interested in (your bid may have to be higher than a certain

Greta von Nessen Anywere lamp for Nessen, Inc., ca. 1952. As the name suggests, this lamp was designed for versatile placement. It can sit on a table or hang on a wall. *Photo courtesy of Wright.*

percentage of the low estimate). Once the auction is underway, the bid will be executed as if you were there.

A better strategy, however, is to ask if you can bid by phone. Phone bidding lets you participate live in the auction and possibly avoid the heartbreak of losing out on an item that went for just slightly more than your absentee bid. Established auction houses have several phone lines manned by staff who will call you when

A variety of Charles and Ray Eames chairs for Herman Miller,
including shell, molded plywood, and secretarial chairs.
Photo courtesy of Wright.

your desired lot comes up and will then stay on the line with you during the bidding, acting as your proxy to place bids up to your maximum.

What's Involved in Claiming My Winnings?

You may pick up the items you win at the auction house following the auction or, in many cases, have them shipped to you. The auction house usually will have laid out the specific guidelines they use to ship merchandise; by registering and thus signing the agreement, you're bound to abide by those guidelines. You shouldn't even think of not honoring your winning bid. When you bid on items, you enter a legal contract to purchase them at the agreed price, and you'll be held to your agreement. In some cases, auctioneers may be willing to arrange short-term storage for a fee (determine this beforehand when you register to bid if it's a necessity for you). But most of the time you should be prepared to remove or arrange for immediate shipment of your winnings. And remember, once the gavel drops and you've won an item, legal title transfers to you. Any damage or loss beyond that point is your responsibility—short of the auctioneer's staff damaging the piece in removing it from the platform.

What Are the Pros and Cons of Buying at a Live Auction?

In today's market, some of the very best pieces are sold at live auctions. But competition can be fierce, as evidenced by the astronomical prices sometimes seen at auctions. But just as every auction has items that sell for far too much, every auction also has its share of outright bargains. Be prepared and patient, and you'll find those bargains!

'50s Decor
Photo Gallery

Arne Jacobsen Egg chair and stool for Knoll, 1958. *Photo courtesy of Knoll.*

George Nelson slat bench for Herman Miller, 1955. A redesign of Nelson's well-known slat bench, this version replaces the original's wooden base with metal legs. *Photo courtesy of Wright.*

Marco Zanuso sofa for Arflex, 1950s. At 96" long, this curving sofa could easily be overwhelming, but the simple, angular legs give it a light feel. The original upholstery has been replaced. *Photo courtesy of Wright.*

George Nelson cube chairs for Herman Miller. *Photo courtesy of Herman Miller, Inc.*

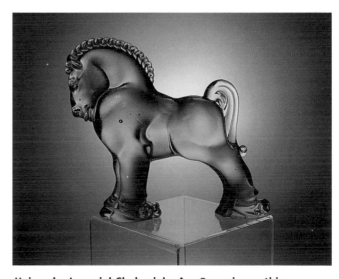

Heisey by Imperial Clydesdale. A 1980s reissue, this design was originally sold by the Heisey Glass Company in the 1940s and early '50s. *Photo courtesy of the National Heisey Glass Museum.*

Hans Wegner cabinet, teak and woven cane, c. 1958. This Danish piece is marked with an identifying brand. The upper doors slide apart to reveal adjustable shelves. *Photo courtesy of Wright.*

Charles and Ray Eames rocker for Zenith Plastics, Herman Miller, 1951. The off-white Zenith shell includes the early rope edge and rests on a base of black wire and birch runners. *Photo courtesy of Wright.*

George Nelson coffee table for Herman Miller, 1955. This rare birch table features a storage area underneath the sliding top and a cantilevered planter with copper insert. The chartreuse tabletop is laminate. *Photo courtesy of Wright.*

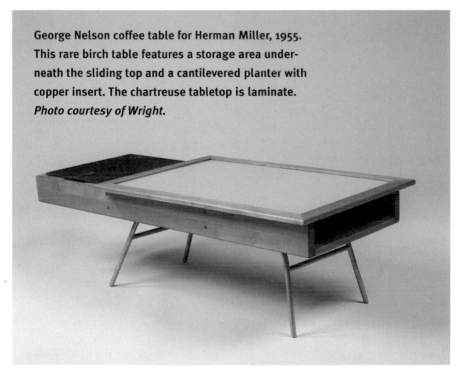

53

Greta Grossman end tables for Glenn of California, 1950s. These two-tiered geometric tables include a contrasting ball at the bottom of each leg. *Photo courtesy of Wright.*

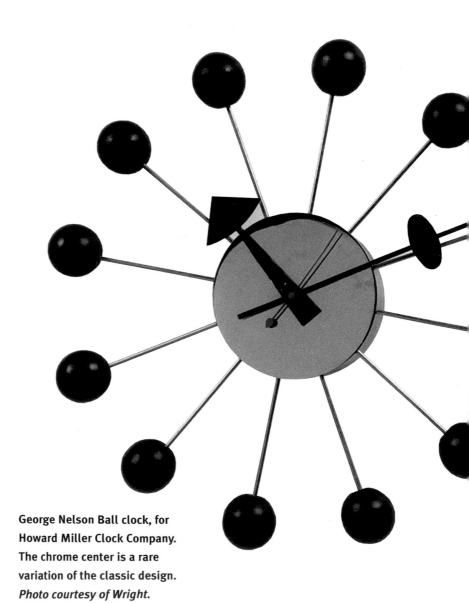

George Nelson Ball clock, for Howard Miller Clock Company. The chrome center is a rare variation of the classic design. *Photo courtesy of Wright.*

Massimo Vigneli hanging lamp shade for Venini, 1950s. Bold stripes from the Fasce series of vases glow on this opaque white shade. *Photo courtesy of Wright.*

Marion Geller floor lamp for Heifetz, 1951. Another entry in the Museum of Modern Art Low Cost Lighting Competition of 1951, this lamp's tilting shade reflects light from the metal cone. *Photo courtesy of Wright.*

Bertrand Goldberg desk, custom-made for a Chicago residence in 1952. This ash veneer and steel piece is typical of the architect's early designs. *Photo courtesy of Wright.*

Poul Kjærholm PK-20 lounge chairs for Fritz Hansen. A cantilevered, stainless steel frame supports the channeled black leather seats. *Photo courtesy of Wright.*

George Nakashima Frenchman's Cove II dining table. Made with solid slabs of walnut, this table features exquisite rosewood butterfly joinery. *Photo courtesy of Wright.*

Charles and Ray Eames upholstered wire chairs on various bases for Herman Miller: wooden four-leg, Eiffel Tower, cat in the cradle, metal four-leg, and rocker. *Photo courtesy of Herman Miller, Inc.*

Charles and Ray Eames DCW chair for Herman Miller, 1950. Highly valued by collectors, this rather impractical slunk-skin version of the classic DCW chair is difficult to find in good condition. *Photo courtesy of Wright.*

57

Paavo Tynell chandelier for Taito (Finland), 1948–1953. Mesh flowers suspended from thin brass wires cast shadows in this fanciful, floral-themed brass chandelier. It was handmade, and due to the expense, very few were produced. *Photo courtesy of Wright.*

Paavo Tynell floor lamp for Taito (Finland). This lamp is topped by a delicate array of mesh foliage, while an adjustable downlight offers illumination for reading. *Photo courtesy of Wright.*

Charles and Ray Eames molded plywood chair for Herman Miller, a 1994 reintroduction of the original design. *Photo by Phil Schaafsma; courtesy of Herman Miller, Inc.*

Gio Ponti console table and Carlo di Carli armchair for Singer and Sons, walnut and brass. The top of the table unfolds to create a small dining table; the chair retains its original upholstery. *Photo courtesy of Wright.*

Ralph Rapson rocker for Knoll Associates, 1945. Rapson studied architecture at Cranbrook Academy, where he became friends with Charles Eames and Eero Saarinen. This birch and canvas-webbed rocker is the most famous of his furniture designs. *Photo courtesy of Wright.*

Hans Wegner dining table and chairs for Fritz Hansen. The table is plywood on a beech frame, the stacking chairs are solid beech with seats of teak veneer. *Photo courtesy of Wright.*

Harry Bertoia Diamond chair for Knoll. *Photo courtesy of Knoll.*

1999 Herman Miller reintro-
duction of the famous
Marshmallow sofa. See page
85 for a view of the original.
*Photo courtesy of Herman
Miller, Inc.*

Edward Wormley sofa for
Dunbar. Retaining its original
lush red upholstery, this sofa
is signed in the decking of the
cushions. *Photo courtesy of
Wright.*

George Nelson cabinet for Howard Miller, 30"L x 18½" w x 22"h. A rosewood cabinet with single drawer on an x-base, this unique piece was never put into production. *Photo courtesy of Wright.*

George Nelson Pretzel
chair for Herman Miller,
made of molded birch.
*Photo courtesy of Herman
Miller, Inc.*

NOW THAT YOU'RE READY TO START COLLECTING

You've read this far and are convinced that collecting Mid-Century Modern is for you. But before you rush out the door, checkbook in hand, take a moment to arm yourself with some inside information (and a few tools) that will help you find the best pieces and get the most for your money.

The Collector's Toolbox

When experienced collectors go to antiques shows and flea markets, they take along much more than their checkbook. These tools can help you evaluate a piece and then transport it safely home if you decide to make it yours.

- **Value guides and catalogs.** The collector's most useful tool is knowledge. But until you've gained more experience, value guides and catalogs are the next best thing. Leave them in your car, and when you find an item you like but are uncertain of, you can always make a quick trip back to look it up. Although sometimes the item will be gone when you return, these little reference jaunts can save you money when they keep you from impulsively buying pieces that are overpriced.

- **Flashlight.** As a beginning collector, some of the first places you'll look for items of interest are garage sales and flea markets. The best of these often start before most noncollectors even wake up, so don't forget your flashlight. When a tiny chip may decide whether an item is worth a fair amount of money or should be thrown away, you don't want to be buying in the dark. A flashlight is a valuable tool in any venue to do a close examination of almost any kind of item. Shop or mall lighting may not be brilliant enough to show up the true condition of a finish or to see the inside or underside of a piece.

- **Camera, notebook, and tape measure.** Affordably priced, easy-to-use point-and-shoot cameras make it simple to take pictures of a piece in which you're interested to serve as a visual reference for further research on the design/manufacturer, dating, condition, value, etc. Use your tape measure to record the measurements for later research, and to get an approximate idea of how the piece will fit into your living space. Etiquette requires that you get the seller's permission before photographing or measuring a piece.

- **Small tool kit.** A portable tool kit with screwdrivers, pliers, and a combination socket set are often handy, and you can't always count on a dealer to have them. You never know when you'll end up with a piece that's too large to fit into the car or van without some minor disassembly.

- **Tote bag and belt pack.** Remember, you're not at a shopping mall—many sellers don't have bags with them. Taking your own tote bag is especially important at larger flea markets, where you may have to park some distance away. And if you're not especially concerned about making a fashion statement, a zippered belt pack for your money, business cards, and receipts will save you the hassle of riffling through your wallet or purse to retrieve and file these things.

- **Wrapping materials.** Also be sure to take some type of wrapping for your items—packing supplies can be hard to come by in the field. Newsprint, bubble wrap, and even paper towels can help protect your newfound treasures. (Just because the person you bought them from didn't think they were valuable enough to protect doesn't mean they're not!) Wrap items carefully, especially if you're packing several fragile pieces in the same bag.

- **Moving blankets.** Keep a moving blanket or two in the trunk of your car to cushion larger pieces you've bought. They'll also keep your bags and smaller items from rolling around on your trip home.

Cash—Don't Leave Home Without It

Always take along ample cash. At garage sales and flea markets, cash is king and sometimes is the only method of payment accepted. Even when it's not, paying with cash—just like offering to buy several items at a "package" price—can be a helpful negotiating strategy if you're interested in bargaining with a dealer. Of course, also take along your checkbook and credit cards. You'll be surprised how many people will accept personal checks, letting you conserve your cash for another purchase or a late breakfast.

At a flea market or antiques show, the competition is all gathered at one time, and you run the risk of losing a desirable piece if you don't move decisively. Etiquette compels other interested parties to keep their distance as long as you're examining a piece or discussing it with the dealer (professional dealers will deflect intrusions most of the time). So take your time and glean as much from the piece as you can. If your gut instincts are at odds with the particulars of the piece and the terms of the transaction, walk away.

Finally, when you're scouting sales and shops far from home, don't forget to pack a map of the area and copies of your "want list." Use the map to plan other stops in the vicinity so you can take advantage of as many sales and buying opportunities as possible. And leave copies of your want list with dealers so they can contact you if they come across something you're looking for.

(Impulse) Buyer Beware

Novice collectors in any field—with more enthusiasm than experience—may be tempted to rush out and purchase every item that catches their eye. Especially for collectors of Mid-Century Modern who didn't grow up in the era, every piece may seem unique and every marked price may seem to represent the "true value." But before making a substantial purchase, make sure you've done your homework. There are many books on Mid-Century collecting that can help. And when an item truly seems underpriced, try to rule out all the possible reasons why—such as reproduction, restoration, concealed damage, etc. Let patience and common sense be your guides. The once-in-a-lifetime find you force yourself to pass up today may well show up again and again, quite possibly in better condition and for less money.

What Determines the Value of a Piece?

Finding pieces you'd like to add to your collection is easy. Finding them at the right price takes a bit more work. Each of the following attributes has some impact on a piece's value—and therefore the price you'll pay.

Condition

Collectors of Mid-Century Modern are in luck: Most of the items they prize so highly were mass-produced not even 50 years ago. So a patient collector stands a good chance of finding pieces in very good to excellent condition, at fair to modest prices.

George Nelson Sling sofa for Herman Miller. *Photo courtesy of Herman Miller, Inc.*

To Refinish or Not To Refinish

As a general rule, a piece that's been refinished or restored is worth only about half as much as an original example. In terms of retaining value, it's always best if you can get by with just a gentle cleaning to keep a piece in service. But for some of the items you'll come across, that won't be enough. For example, few collectors would be interested in a George Nelson credenza with original but peeling paint. Taking the piece to a refinisher who's familiar with the design and can restore it to its original condition would be the best course of action. In that instance, given the state of the original piece, refinishing can *add* to its value as a collectible.

In the field of ceramics, pottery, and glass, condition is paramount. A tiny nick that's barely noticeable or a hairline crack that can be seen only at a certain angle can dramatically affect a piece's desirability and value. Even defects that originated in the manufacture of an item can devalue it. Some pieces with glaze misses, glass bubbles, and poorly applied appliqués were originally sold as "seconds" by discounters because they weren't deemed acceptable for sale through normal distribution channels. Seconds sometimes can be identified by the absence of the company's usual hallmark on the piece.

With furniture, condition standards are a bit more relaxed. Of course, a piece that's in the same condition as when it was made still is the ultimate standard. But much postwar furniture was made to be accessible to the masses, not just the elite as in prior eras, and pieces saw daily use. Many collectors appreciate signs of normal wear, preferring a piece with a small chip or scratch to one that's been refinished or restored.

Of course, sometimes a bit of restoration is inevitable to maintain a piece's appearance or usability—the replacement of worn upholstery fabric, for example. Many designs from the period used latex foam for its wonderful sculptural qualities. Over time, the foam hardens and disintegrates into powder.

In the end, each collector must decide for himself just how much importance to assign to condition. If you have the money and are looking only for value appreciation in the pieces you buy, then hold out for original-condition examples. On the other hand, if you simply want to decorate your home with beautiful objects at affordable prices, you'll find a range of choices waiting for you.

69

Damage

Collecting Mid-Century Modern can be a bit confounding where damage is concerned. Many Mid-Century pieces were relegated to damp basements or garages when they went out of fashion, incurring various types of damage in the process. And because of the simplicity of most pieces, damage of any kind becomes fairly prominent and may be hard to disguise or camouflage.

In general, look for pieces that appear to have been cared for their whole life. And never forget to factor in how you plan to use a piece. For example, if you're looking for dinnerware to display as showpieces in your collection, nothing short of perfect condition may do. But if your plan is to use the pieces every day and make them part of your lifestyle, a bit of light crazing or a few small chips won't be a problem and even may add to their charm.

As you shop, be on the lookout for common types of damage:

- **Wood damage.** Many Mid-Century case goods used wood veneer or a combination of veneers and solid wood. Chipped or water-damaged veneer is a common problem and, unfortunately, one that can be costly to repair. Significant damage to solid-wood components usually requires fabricating a replacement part.

- **Upholstery damage.** Pieces with their original upholstery intact and exhibiting only light wear or soiling are prized for good reason. Upholstered pieces are subject to a range of maladies: worn, torn, or faded fabrics (red fabrics seem most susceptible to fading); deteriorated or hardened foam rubber; and broken or loose springs and webbing.

- **Stains and discoloration.** In general, avoid pieces with wood finishes that have been heavily stained by oil, grease, or paint—repairing this kind of damage usually requires restoration. If a piece has plastic components, make sure any surface discoloration hasn't penetrated the plastic itself, in which case it probably can't be removed.

- **Sun damage.** Wood pieces will fade or bleach and even dry out with prolonged exposure to direct sunlight. Plastics are especially susceptible to sun damage, and the resulting discoloration is permanent.

- **Water damage.** Water is a highly interactive substance that can cause great damage to wood, metal, plastics, and fabrics. Small water spots on wood finishes can be removed if they're objectionable, but if they're a sign of hidden problems such as loose veneer, mildew, or rot, the piece may not be worth owning. Rust on metal components that hasn't progressed beyond the "patina" stage may be acceptable. But if water damage has advanced to the point where surfaces are pitted, aluminum finishes are corroded, or chrome plating is loose or flaked, the piece has serious problems. If chrome components don't clean up acceptably with a light rubbing of very fine steel wool, expensive rechroming may be the only option.
- **Finish or paint deterioration.** Badly worn wood or metal finishes always detract from a piece's value. Before investing in such a piece, make sure you understand how restoration will affect its value.

With experience, you'll be able to evaluate these kinds of damage and sort out negligible instances from the true sale-breakers. For help, study books on specific Mid-Century collectibles, as well as price guides and auction catalogs. Well written descriptions in auction catalogs detail all specific damage and defects, as well as the overall condition of the pieces offered. If you purchase a catalog, the auction house will likely send you a list of the prices that the items realized. This will give you a good idea of how various kinds of damage may affect comparative values.

Missing or Replaced Parts

An item that has all of its original components is almost always worth more than a similar one that's incomplete or has had parts replaced. But this is very much a judgment call. Is a missing screw reason enough to pass on an otherwise wonderful piece? Probably not. And minor replacement parts such as floor glides shouldn't adversely affect a piece's value if they have the same specifications as the originals.

However, if one or several major parts are reproductions—such as chair legs or tabletops—the piece may be worth substantially less. Every collector must decide at what point too many replacement parts make the piece a reproduction and no longer the original. Of course, if you simply like it as-is and aren't really concerned about its value as a collectible, then it's probably a piece you should buy if the price is right.

Second-Hand Clocks

Sometimes, the tiniest replacement part is the one that has the biggest effect on value. Consider the George Nelson–designed wall clocks that were produced by the Howard Miller Clock Company. The popularity of these clocks has skyrocketed, along with the prices they bring. A problem with the original design, however, caused the second hand to twist off after a period of use. That's why today it's rare to find one of these clocks with an original second hand. If you do, expect to pay a premium of 25 to 30 percent. It's a bit ironic, but a second hand that cost only pennies to produce can add as much as several hundred dollars to the price of the clock!

Functionality

What if the item you'd like to buy no longer works? Is it still worth owning, and if so, at what price?

This is another judgment call. If the item is collectible primarily because of the way it operates (such as a mechanical bank or a television), then the fact that it's no longer functional should substantially reduce its value and the price you pay.

On the other hand, if the item is prized more for its design or rarity (George Nelson clocks are a good example), then a piece that's in good physical condition even if mechanically broken may be worth nearly as much as one that works. Such items, in effect, have transcended the category of mechanical conveniences to become works of art. They now exist for their own sake, with only a nod to their former function.

Repairs and Restoration

Most collectors readily buy pieces that have been repaired to some degree. Especially with furniture, some degree of repair is almost inevitable—scratches have been touched up or veneer chips filled. Repaired furniture pieces usually are slightly less valuable than their perfect counterparts but usually more valuable than if the repairs hadn't been made.

A piece that's been restored to its original condition without the addition of any new materials is still a good investment and should be worth only slightly less than an unrestored version. Often, though, a restoration is more extensive and may involve refinishing, reveneering, repainting, reupholstering, or, if there are metal components, replating. A piece that has had extensive refabrication or replacement of parts is significantly less valuable.

Restorations aren't always easy to spot (except ones that are poorly done). Always ask the dealer what he knows about the history of the piece, with specific emphasis on its condition and any repairs or restoration the dealer is aware of. Then take the time to look the piece over completely. The underside will often yield clues. If the piece was restored, drip marks on the underside may show where stripper or finish was applied. If the piece was reupholstered, the underside often retains signs of the original fabric.

T.H. Robsjohn-Gibbings sofa for Widdicomb. This elegant sofa features a walnut frame and brass legs. The design dates to the mid-fifties. *Photo courtesy of Wright.*

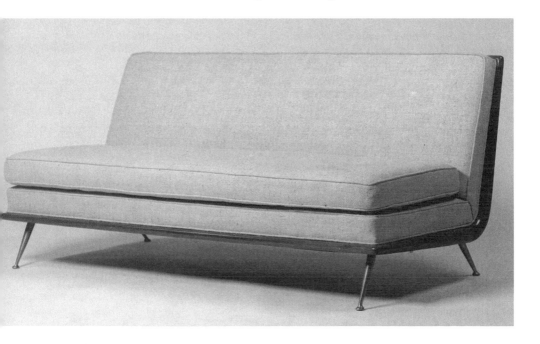

Also look for these signs that a piece may have been restored:

- Thick, uneven wood finishes.
- Patched or mismatched veneers.
- Runny or pebbly paint finishes.
- Parts that don't appear to have as much wear as others.
- A strong chemical smell from newly applied paint or finish.

What a Black Light Reveals

Much more so than with furniture, even expert repairs to glass, ceramics, and pottery can cause the value to plummet. What's more, these repairs can be very hard to spot. That's why some collectors insist on viewing these items under a long-wave black light. It's often the only way some expert repairs can be detected. (Don't bother packing a black light to take to flea markets or shows. And because most dealers will accept returned items, it's rarely necessary to take one to specialty shops, either.)

A black light produces ultraviolet rays that react with the surface of an item. Different materials absorb ultraviolet rays at different rates and so will stand out. When you look at an item under a black light, it's these differences you're looking for. If there's new paint, it will appear to glow under a black light. Likewise, a hairline crack that was invisible under normal light will be readily apparent.

Original Packaging

Unlike collectible toys and dolls, most items of Mid-Century Modern aren't significantly more valuable if their boxes or original packaging are intact. In fact, it's unlikely that you'll find many offered for sale that way. Still, there are some avid collectors who place a high value on original boxes as collectible ephemera.

When you do find an item in its original box, however, it may be an indication that the item was seldom if ever used or was especially well cared for. In that case, the item may indeed be more valuable, but not simply because of the box. Complete sets of collectible dinnerware still in their original boxes sometimes sell at premium prices.

Original Labels and Stickers

A label is simply a sticker or stamp put on a piece by its original manufacturer to identify his goods. Although many collectors have a preference for labeled pieces, the label itself doesn't greatly add to the value. Don't make the mistake of passing by an otherwise outstanding example just because it lacks a label (or a signature).

The Icing on the Cake

The original owners of postwar furniture usually were given sales material such as catalogs and brochures at the time of purchase. The furniture of George Nakashima almost always came with a design sketch along with the sales receipt (as it still does today).

A surprising number of owners held on to these things, and occasionally you'll find pieces for sale that include these original documents. Such material is best viewed as icing on the cake— little extras that add to a piece's history and interest but little to its value.

Many early or rare pieces of postwar furniture were unsigned, and the very earliest examples of Eames chairs predate the labels that were designed to go on them.

A label can be important, however, when it helps approximate the production date of an item. Many manufacturers altered their labels over time. If a piece enjoyed a long production run—20 years or more—the appearance of the label can help identify the earliest examples. And these are often the ones most valued by collectors.

The Eames molded plywood chair is a classic example of a piece for which the label is key. Before Herman Miller, Inc., began to manufacture this design, it was produced by a company called Evans Products. Early chairs that retain the Evans label can be worth several hundred dollars more than the newer Herman Miller models.

Intrinsic Characteristics

So just what is it that makes one Mid-Century piece an item that collectors seek out but another an also-ran? There are probably as many answers as there are collectors, but here are some of the things that strike a common chord:

- **Design icons.** These are the famous pieces from top designers that, over time, have achieved icon status. Examples include the Eames plywood chairs, the Noguchi glass-top coffee table, and the George Nelson Ball clock and Marshmallow sofa. All of these items represent a turning point in design or the crystallization of a new design idea and so are perennially popular with collectors.

Two Eames sofas with a Noguchi glass-topped table, for Herman Miller. *Photo courtesy of Herman Miller, Inc.*

- **Pieces with designer attribution.** Designers became extremely important during this time, and many architects began to produce furniture designs. Collectors are as likely to look for a specific designer as much as for a specific style. But although a particular designer's name associated with a piece can be worth money, even the best designers had a few "duds." Many novice collectors make the mistake of buying pieces with a designer name not realizing that they have little or no collectible value.

- **Examples of biomorphic or kidney-shaped design.** Although many of these pieces were kitschy in nature, even well-respected designers reflected this style. Isamu Noguchi's sculptural coffee table for Herman Miller and Frederick Weinberg's backlit wall sculptures are familiar examples.

- **Clean, functional designs.** Durable, well-constructed pieces with clean lines and little ornamentation were popularized by designers such as Charles and Ray Eames, George Nelson, and Florence Knoll.

- **Unusual items.** The mid-century was a time of great experimentation that yielded lots of odd and quirky items—from lamps with furry fiberglass shades to starburst lighting fixtures. Many collectors are drawn to these unusual items that are outside the history of design, and rare items in this category are as eagerly sought as the upscale design icons, albeit at much lower prices.

Age

With Mid-Century Modern, "age of production" has more impact on a piece's value than "age of design." In other words, a piece from 1945 isn't inherently more valuable than one from 1958—but it could be *more* valuable if 1945 happened to be the first year it was produced rather than the fifteenth. Even for pieces that are still in production and may be available from the original manufacturer, most collectors will seek out earlier examples.

Vintage pieces are valued for their:

- **Scarcity.** Often, early variants were produced in shorter production runs.

- **Attrition.** Earlier pieces are survivors—they weren't lost or destroyed.
- **Design changes.** Later examples may have been "improved" by material or hardware changes.
- **Patina.** Earlier examples may have a richer or more desirable appearance; they don't feel "new."

So how can you tell if a particular piece is an earlier example and not simply a current but faithful reissue or reproduction? Start with . . . .

- **Manufacturers' labels.** Most manufacturers change the design of their labels over time. Dealers and specialty reference books can help you spot the differences.
- **Manufacturers' catalogs.** This is primary source material—and the least subject to errors—and is invaluable for collectors who like to do their own research. Original catalogs are nice (and may be collectible in their own right), but the increasingly available reprints are just as helpful.
- **Published references.** Publications such as *Echoes* magazine and *Modernism* magazine regularly run articles on design variations that can help you date a piece.
- **Dealer claims or estimations.** Dealers are a great source of information, but collectors should be wary of any age claim used as a selling tool. A dealer should be willing to put all claims in writing; your receipt should indicate the approximate age of the example you're buying.
- **Stylistic references.** Although it takes a bit of knowledge and experience to use, an understanding of the styles that were broadly in fashion at different times can give you clues to a piece's age.
- **Materials.** Some materials, such as plywood, Masonite, and rubber, are signatures of their era. In an older piece, you're more likely to find solid steel (instead of a lighter material) and rubber mounts and foot pads (instead of plastic).
- **Signs of age.** Learning to spot the effects of time on certain materials such as wood, metal, and paint can help you decide whether the age that's claimed for a piece "feels" right.
- **Patent numbers.** Often found on the underside of furniture,

a patent number will sometimes be the only information you'll have when dating an unknown piece. But in most cases, it will date only the design (or perhaps just one part of the design, such as its table leaves) and not the age of the particular example you're considering.

One of the reasons collecting Mid-Century Modern is so exciting is that its history is still being written and discovered. You may have to comb more sources to piece together the information you're looking for, but the search is what will make your eventual purchases all the more special.

Rarity

In any field of collecting, the rarest examples are the collector's treasure. Mid-Century Modern has created its share of rarities, but these rarities didn't all achieve that status for the same reason.

- **Some were commercial flops.** The postwar era was a wonderful time in America when many large furniture manufacturers were willing to take chances on extreme designs. Would a small stool that was meant to rock like a rocking chair be practical to mass-produce? Knoll apparently thought so when they introduced the rocking stool by Isamu Noguchi. Its limited practicality and resulting lack of sales are the very things that make it so rare and prized today.

- **Some were too fragile or deemed too plain.** Although Eames Storage Units were produced in great number, the early examples were somewhat fragile: Their frames would bend under a load. And their low-end materials—Masonite, plywood, and steel—prompted many owners to relegate them to the basement or garage when they were no longer new. As a result, early examples in original condition are hard to find.

- **Some were custom designs.** Custom-made furniture is inherently rare. The architect Richard Neutra's furniture—designed expressly for specific interiors—is an example.

- **Some were rarities by intent.** Unique and one-of-a-kind designs are the rarest of the rare—and their prices reflect that status. The price record for a Mid-Century piece is held by a Charles and Ray Eames plywood sculpture: $360,000. This piece was an experiment in form not intended for production, and probably no more than three were ever made.

Two Eames lounge chairs with ottomans; the woman is seated in a 684 lounge chair and the man in the 670. *Photo courtesy of Herman Miller, Inc.*

Production variations also may make a particular piece rare but not necessarily more valuable. For example, the classic version of the Eames 670 lounge chair and ottoman was produced in black leather with rosewood veneer. Some chairs, however, were made in custom leather colors such as blue, orange, and white. Although rare, they're not as aesthetically pleasing to collectors as a black-leather model in great original condition.

Prototypes and pieces that were altered or redesigned during production are a different story, however. Prototypes are almost always a desirable investment—so much so that they're usually handled by large auction houses that specialize in 20th-century modern. And when a piece undergoes a design change, the early version may become much more desirable. Early production of the Eames Fiberglass Shell chair incorporated a nylon rope embedded in the outer lip of the molded piece. But it was eliminated within the first two years due to manufacturing problems.

Trying to pin down a piece's rarity can be confounding even to experienced collectors. It can take years of collecting—decades even—to gain a thorough overview of the period. In the meantime, consult as many sources as you can:

- **Auctions** have resulted in a vast record of rare pieces that have sold and the prices they brought. Dealers such as Catalog Kid specialize in selling back issues of auction catalogs.
- **Dealers** will have seen many more pieces than you have and may be able to tell you if the example you're considering is rare. Ask several—not just the one offering the item for sale—where they've seen similar pieces and when. Find out how often they'd expect this piece to surface.

Hans Wegner Valet chair for Johannes Hansen, c. 1953. Fashioned from teak, leather, and brass, this unusual chair doubles as a clothes rack: the chair back can be used as a jacket or shirt hanger, the seat lifts to form a pant hanger, and a small storage space under the seat holds pocket contents. *Photo courtesy of Wright.*

- **Manufacturers** sometimes provide the best and most accurate information. Although some may have gone out of business or kept sketchy records, others still may be operating and producing the same designs. Some persistent collectors have even tracked down the people who worked on a particular design to ascertain its rarity.

- **The Internet** contains a wealth of information on all aspects of collecting. Collecting bulletin boards can put you in touch with others who may know about the rarity of a particular piece. As with most information on the Web, however, you should use your own judgment in separating fact from opinion.

Attribution

The hands that touched an item can have a big impact on its value, and Mid-Century works by known designers typically sell for the highest prices and retain the highest values. (That's not to say, however, that undocumented works by less well-known designers may not be good investments.) Before paying a premium price based primarily on the association of a piece with the designer's name, insist on definitive documentation—an illustration of the piece in a primary source book such as a manufacturer's catalog, for example. Look-alike works "in the style of" a particular designer or "attributed to" a particular designer are plentiful, and although many of these pieces are desirable, they're not as valuable as a well-documented original.

Consider yourself lucky if you find one of these definitive signs of attribution:

- **Initials or a signature.** On art pottery and ceramics, initials on the bottom of a piece signify that a specific designer produced it. A full signature on the front of some ceramics, such as those by Sascha Brastoff, indicates that the designer hand-painted the item himself. Such pieces can command many times the price of those made by other designers who merely worked under his direction.

- **A manufacturer's label or the designer's name.** On a piece of furniture, these are be located in an inconspicuous area, if they're still present at all.

More often, you'll have to settle for building a case of "strong attribution" by sleuthing for clues like:

- **A factory mark.** Knowing that a piece was made at the same place where a given designer worked is a good starting point in determining attribution.
- **Stylistic elements.** Do parts of the piece match another design that's documented to be the designer's work? Designers often worked in related styles, repeating a leg detail or drawer-pull design, for example.
- **Model numbers.** Familiarize yourself with the model numbers commonly used by the manufacturer. Sometimes they're present when nothing else remains to identify a piece. Reprints of manufacturers' catalogs are good sources for model numbers.
- **The piece's history.** If you're dealing with the original owners, don't hesitate to ask where a piece of furniture came from. If you're talking with a dealer, he may be able to put you in touch with the previous owners.

Provenance

Is the value of a piece enhanced simply because of who's owned it in the past? As the record prices seen at recent celebrity auctions attest, the answer is often yes. However, new collectors should view the provenance of a piece as the cherry on a sundae—a nice addition but not the main feature. The underlying quality of the piece is key; an inferior item from a great collection is still an inferior item.

Of particular interest, however, are items that were personally owned by the designer (or his family and friends). Items that come from a designer's estate often command prices that far exceed those of their more commonplace counterparts—perhaps because they tend to be originals, but also because the designer himself deemed them desirable enough to include in his own collection.

As a collector, you'll likely have to rely on the dealer or auctioneer for accurate and truthful information about the provenance of a piece. Letters of provenance from the original owners or their families, along with photographs and invoices, are the most

COLLECTOR'S COMPASS

TM

Names to Know

Although there are countless great designs by lesser-known designers, the shining lights of Mid-Century Modern are all comparatively well known:

UNITED STATES

Harry Bertoia—sculptor and furniture designer who studied at Cranbrook. His wire chairs are produced by Knoll and have become icons of the era.

Charles and Ray Eames—husband and wife creative team who became a wellspring of Mid-Century design, especially while working at Herman Miller.

Alexander Girard—textile and interior designer who worked for Herman Miller. He was a great friend of the Eameses and is known for his striking use of color and pattern.

Florence Knoll—furniture designer who studied at Cranbrook and formed (with her husband Hans Knoll) Knoll Furniture. Knoll still produces outstanding designer furniture.

George Nakashima—woodworker from New Hope, Pennsylvania. His furniture is a distinctive combination of the craft tradition with modern design. His studio is still in existence and is run by his daughter Mira.

George Nelson—design director for Herman Miller who brought Charles Eames and Noguchi to Miller. He ran a prolific design studio that produced many classics of the era, such as the Marshmallow sofa, Coconut chair, and clocks for Howard Miller.

Isamu Noguchi—famous sculptor who designed furniture for Herman Miller and Knoll.

Eero Saarinen—son of the famous Finnish architect Eliel Saarinen. He studied at Cranbrook with Charles Eames. His important furniture designs include the Womb and Grasshopper chairs (done for Knoll). As an architect, he designed the famous TWA terminal in Washington, D.C., and the St. Louis Arch.

ITALY

Carlo Mollino—exotic and distinctive architect and designer. His work is the most visually extreme of the era. Almost all of his furniture was custom made for specific interiors, making it quite rare and expensive.

Ico Parisi—furniture designer.

Gio Ponti—architect and designer active in Italy from 1920 to 1970. He was the editor of the influential *Domus* magazine.

FRANCE

Jean Prouvé—architect and furniture designer known for his use of industrial materials (primarily steel).

SCANDINAVIA

Arne Jacobsen—architect and furniture designer.

Poul Kjærholm—architect and furniture designer.

Hans Wegner—architect and furniture designer.

left: Designed in 1956 by Irving Harper of George Nelson and Associates, the Marshmallow sofa has 18 cushions that can be individually cleaned or replaced.

widely accepted forms of documentation. If the piece came from an auction, keep the catalog (get an extra copy to stay with the piece) and the lot-number sticker. If it's from a museum, retain the tag or code number that identified the piece. Try to get the history of the piece in writing, signed by someone who can verify it (and not just the dealer who's selling the piece).

Dealing with Knock-Offs, Fakes, Reproductions, and Reissues

A knock-off is an unauthorized copy of a piece in which the design is altered (usually cheapened) in order to avoid paying royalties to the designer or his estate. Most knock-offs are of little interest to collectors. There are several variations of the Eames lounge chair and ottoman, for example, and a beginning collector may not immediately be able to spot a knock-off. But once you've had the opportunity to examine one or two originals, you'll notice that most knock-offs have a four-star (four-pronged) base, not the five-star base of the original. You'll also see that the materials used in most copies are noticeably inferior to the leather upholstery and rosewood veneer in the Eames model (later and current versions no longer use rosewood but the quality of the wood is still evident). As you begin collecting, it's best to walk away from a piece if you have any doubts about its authenticity.

The Eero Saarinen pedestal table and chairs have also spawned many knock-offs. Various company names appear on the copies, the most familiar being Burke of Texas. The knock-offs often use screws to attach the pedestal base to the top; no screws are visible on the original because the base screws directly to the top. Such copies normally are clearly identified and aren't intended to masquerade as originals, but new collectors should be on the alert. You don't want to pay a Saarinen price for a Burke table.

Fakes are a bit more difficult to spot because their intent is to deceive. Fakes are often priced at about half of what the original piece would be worth, making them seem like a bargain to a novice buyer. If you're ever drawn to such an example, specifically ask the seller: Is this item old? Is it original? If the seller is reluctant to put all claims in writing or to accept a check, be on guard. As a new

collector, try to limit major purchases to established dealers and auction houses that guarantee their items.

Reproductions and reissues of some classic designs are currently available from companies such as Herman Miller and Knoll, but whether these new items eventually will have the collector appeal and value of the originals is a subject of debate. Because Mid-Century Modern is such a young field of collecting, some experts contend that it's still relatively easy to build a collection with original items without having to resort to reproductions.

1994 Herman Miller Inc. reintroduction of the classic Noguchi coffee table. Photo courtesy of Herman Miller, Inc.

Building Your Collection

Novice collectors of Mid-Century Modern often walk a tightrope. Their newfound interest and growing knowledge of the field are propelling them into the marketplace, but they're still vexed by questions about everything from deciding what to buy to what to do with their pieces once they own them. If this sounds like you, take heart. Many collectors have asked themselves the same questions and are more than happy to share advice.

How Do I Decide What to Collect?
"Decide" may be the wrong word to use here. Chances are, the decision's already been made for you. What types of pieces have grabbed your attention and just wouldn't let go? What one item did you love at first sight?

The Theme's the Thing
Many collectors choose to build around a particular theme, such as specific items by one designer (Nelson clocks) or manufacturer (Herman Miller furniture). Variations across the theme can help define the collection and provide a context in which to interpret the individual items. For example, one clock by George Nelson may catch your eye, but ten of them on a wall will show you the sheer diversity and experimentation that were involved in their design. In a sense, such a collection "talks to itself."

The nice thing about building a collection around a theme is that there are few hard-and-fast rules. The theme of a collection needn't even be apparent to the viewer: Some outstanding collections have as their only theme the simple fact that all the pieces were assembled by a single person!

The only reason to collect is for the love of it. Passion—pure unadulterated passion—is the most important ingredient in any great collection. Most collectors still can proudly point out their "first buy," and it's usually not an expensive item but simply something that spoke to them. Listen to your heart. Follow your instincts. You may discover that your particular passion is for a certain time period, a certain designer or manufacturer, or just the occasional odd idiosyncratic piece. Whatever it is, embrace it, explore it, and have fun with it.

How Can I Tell Whether I Should Buy
a Particular Piece I Like?

Once you've found *what* you'd like to buy, knowledge is your best ally in deciding *whether* to buy. Certainly, if the piece you're considering carries a high price, you should try to learn as much about it as you can before writing the check. Politely ask the dealer why the piece is priced as it is. Dealers are an invaluable source of information—don't hesitate to ask whatever questions are on your mind. Also ask the dealer for permission to handle the item. Much can be learned just by touching and feeling a piece. You may decide that you need to research the piece further before committing to it. In that case, reference books and magazines from the period can give you a good overview, and there's now a wealth of information on the Internet.

> **If You Think You Can't Afford It, Think Again**
>
> You've just found the perfect example of a piece you know like the back of your hand, the one you thought you'd never find. Your pulse quickens as you approach it. Then the price tag stops—and sinks—your heart. Buying it would put collecting anything else on hold for the rest of the year—maybe longer.
>
> Before you sigh and walk away, consider this sage advice from a collector who's faced the same dilemma. "It's the best items in your collection that will stand the test of time, the ones that have the most to give you. I've learned that the items I stretched the most to buy are the ones that are most special. I had to stretch to buy them because they have an immediacy that made the seller reluctant to sell and a power that made others compete for them. These items have had the most to give."

With more experience, you may conclude, as many seasoned collectors have, that it's wisest to buy the best examples you can afford—to opt for fewer items of higher quality or greater rarity rather than many common items.

How Should I Organize and Display My Pieces?

There are just as many ways to display a collection as there are types of collectibles. Small pieces such as pottery and glass lend themselves to clustered groupings that highlight their similarities and differences. Larger pieces like lamps are perfect for displaying

---

Look . . . and Please Touch!

Don't make the mistake of putting your Mid-Century pieces in "look but don't touch" kinds of displays. Sure, some extremely valuable items probably *should* sit behind glass doors or perhaps even in a specially made display cabinet. But most Mid-Century furniture was meant to be used and lived with, not just admired from afar. And you don't need to create a "period room" to enjoy your collection on a daily basis. Mid-Century Modern integrates beautifully in both contemporary and traditional rooms.

---

throughout the house as a convenient way to integrate the decor. Many collectors of Mid-Century Modern go for the "museum look"—cleaner, leaner arrangements in which individual pieces take center stage. For display ideas, check out *Echoes,* a magazine devoted to Modernism that regularly pictures collectors' personal environments—from period rooms to more contemporary spaces.

How Big Might My Collection Get?

Big. And if you're not careful, really big! Strange as it may seem, some would argue that lucky is the collector who has very limited space and a bank account to match.

Be forewarned: Collecting can become an addiction. Some collectors who've bought more than their house could hold have had to park on the street after commandeering the garage. Others have built entire room additions solely for more storage and display space. If you need yet another reason to subscribe to the "quality vs. quantity" school of collecting, they don't get much better than this!

Should I Try to Collect Broadly or Cherry-Pick for Only the Best Pieces?

Most collectors seem to want the best of both worlds—pieces that represent a good overview of their chosen area as well as the best pieces within that field. The centerpiece items—the "crown jewels" of the collection—are what separates a collection from the rest of the pack and elevates it above the commonplace. After all, possessing a rare item that no one else has is a collector's dream. But even if you're fortunate enough to own such a standout, the more common representative examples that surround it also are an important backdrop to establish a context in which the "stars" can shine. Of course, whether you're considering an item that's a star or one of the supporting players, the touchstone is always: How much do you love it?

A Plethora of Pottery

One collector tells the cautionary tale of his foray into collecting Glidden pottery, a very collectible pottery that was manufactured in Alfred, New York. Assuming (incorrectly) that it would be difficult to find, he bought every piece he came across with the name Glidden etched on the base—and even unmarked items that he believed to be Glidden pottery.

After he'd amassed nearly 1,000 pieces, he began to attend more exclusive shows and for the first time was exposed to an entirely different class of Glidden pottery. "The shapes were more unusual than any I had seen before. The glazes were more remarkable, and many of the items I could only dream of owning. Had I not spent a small fortune on amassing a houseful of less desirable pieces, I probably could have purchased more of these prime examples."

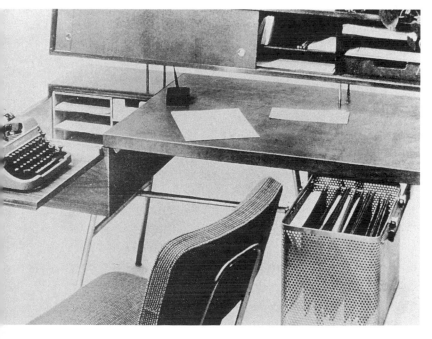

1952 George Nelson Home Office desk with chair. *Photo courtesy of Herman Miller, Inc.*

*Are There Currently Any Bargains
in Mid-Century Collectibles?*

The market for collectibles can be fickle. What once had little value may be highly collectible during a different time. Tastes change, and even the publicity associated with a new book on certain collectibles can generate demand and drive up prices.

So how do you spot the next hot trend? Start by looking at the products created—and then rendered obsolete—by technology. (Were you one of the trend-setters who paid $300 for one of the "new" LED calculators back in the '70s?) Also comb thrift stores and the junkier flea markets and observe what's for sale. Pay special attention to items that embody the time period in which they were made or that visually express their era. If they were made of materials that are no longer used or that are unique, that's another plus. Are there items among the cast-offs that speak to you in a special way or that possess a certain beauty? It may take a collector's eye and a bit of creativity to uncover these hidden gems, but the results can be well worth the effort.

Should You Settle for Less?

There will be times when you'll be tempted to buy a mediocre example of a piece you truly want to acquire simply as a placeholder in your collection until a better one comes along. When this happens, ask yourself how rare the piece really is. If it shows up less than once a year at major auctions or in your dealer network, you very well may have to settle for less than a stellar example. But be sure you're paying accordingly. Remember—when you're eventually ready to trade up, you'll be trying to sell a mediocre item. And that's never an easy thing to do.

---

*How Can I Improve on the Pieces
I've Already Collected?*

One of the joys of collecting is watching your taste change as you gain more knowledge and experience. That item you just had to have a year ago may lose its appeal over time—and that's perfectly all right. You can always sell it. As a beginning collector, don't be afraid to buy some smaller pieces just to get a feel for them. Take them home, live with them for a while, and see if they mesh with your style. If you grow to love them, you may have the start of a collection.

Many dealers started out as collectors who simply wanted to sell their cast-offs. As a collector, you'll always have a need to sell—whether it's to trade up or simply for a change.

What Records Should I Keep?

Tracking down and buying individual pieces is just the start of establishing your Mid-Century collection. As the saying goes, no job is truly complete until the paperwork is done. You'll want to maintain accurate and up-to-date records to document and protect the value of your collection.

- **Receipts.** Just as you keep receipts for major household purchases, you also should retain a dated receipt for each item in your collection. If it's not already noted, add a full description of the item, including its age and condition, the designer's name, its style, shape, color, pattern, size or dimensions, and any distinguishing markings; the name and contact information of the dealer; the date of purchase; and the venue (such as a multivendor flea market). If the seller made any guarantees concerning the item, ask that he note them on the receipt, too, along with his signature.

  Many collectors maintain elaborate notebooks and binders of their collections' documentation, often sprinkled with personal anecdotes about how certain examples were acquired. In its own way, this information may prove as valuable as the items themselves to those who will own them in the future. As one collector observed, "We don't own these items but are only taking care of them for a time."

- **Other documentation.** Letters of provenance and original-owner receipts are valuable documents that will come in handy later in establishing the value of your pieces. If you routinely photograph your pieces upon purchase, keep these snapshots—identified on the back with the purchase date, cost, and dealer name—with this documentation.

- **Dealer contacts.** As a new collector, you'll find that helpful, reputable dealers with whom you've done business or with whom you've simply made contact are among your best assets and are well worth keeping track of. Some may allow you to trade up when they run across a better example of a piece you originally purchased from them. And many work from a "call book" or will keep your want list and search for particular items you're seeking. Always ask for the dealer's business card whenever you make a purchase. If none is available, jot down the dealer's address and phone number on your receipt.

- **Want lists.** Successful collectors make the most of their dealer network by making it as easy as possible for dealers to pinpoint exactly what they want. Maintain want lists of the items you're looking for and make them as specific as possible, including information on designers, manufacturers, and condition, as appropriate. Share them with your dealers—providing regular updates—and don't forget to take multiple copies whenever you go to shows or on shopping expeditions.

Once you've gone to the trouble of recording this information, you'll want to keep it in a safe place. A fireproof box or safe

---

High-Tech Help for Record-Keeping: Your Computer Inventory
Sometimes it's just plain impractical (or impossible) to get a receipt for a purchase. At flea markets, for example, many dealers may not even use a receipt book. In those instances, log the date, purchase price, and the dealer contact information in your pocket notebook. Back home, you'll want to transfer this information to a formal inventory of your collection. And today, that inventory usually is maintained on a personal computer.

Choose a good inventory software program for collectibles, such as Primasoft Collectibles Organizer. In addition to complete descriptions of the items in your collection, many will also let you store scanned images of the photos you've taken. In some ways, this type of electronic archive is superior to storing individual photos in an inventory book or keeping narrated videotapes of your collection. With images captured on compact media such as floppy disks or Zip disks, storage is a snap. And retrieving your images later may be more reliable than with hard-copy photos (which can deteriorate) or videotapes (which can jam or degrade over time). Just be sure to keep backup copies of your computer inventory and update them regularly.

---

is ideal—indeed, some collectors consider it essential. If you keep a computerized inventory, store at least one backup copy off-premises—either at your place of work, in a safe deposit box, or perhaps on a separate computer server.

Do I Need an Appraisal?

You should always know the approximate market value of your items. The value of any piece will fluctuate over time, and it's important to keep up with current valuations—especially when you're about to buy or sell.

But that doesn't necessarily mean you need a professional appraisal. You often can ballpark current values with a quick call to a qualified dealer or auction house. Depending on the size and type of your collection, an appraisal can be expensive, so get one only when there's a genuine need, such as when:

- It's required by your insurance company to ensure adequate coverage.
- You're preparing to sell an item of singularly high value.
- You're dealing with a divorce or estate settlement.
- You're about to donate items for which you'll claim a tax deduction.
- You've just inherited a collection that you have no idea how to value.

COLLECTOR'S COMPASS™

Appraisals 101

An appraisal is simply an expert opinion of the value of a particular item or collection. Dealers and auction houses will often give you a free pre-auction estimate that may have some value, but for a formal written appraisal, you'll need a licensed professional appraiser and you'll pay a fee for his or her services.

An appraisal usually includes:
- A complete description of the item being appraised, including any documentation such as original invoices or letters of provenance.
- Remarks on the item's condition that affect the valuation.
- Notes on additional factors that affect value (such as rarity or previous ownership).
- Current and anticipated market conditions for the specific item.
- An appraisal of the item's current market value.

Mid-Century Modern is still an emerging field for collectibles, so qualified appraisers may be difficult to find. You're more likely to find appraisers who have experience with a wide range of antiques but only limited exposure to Mid-Century Modern. Qualify the appraisers you interview for their specific expertise with Mid-Century pieces, and never make the mistake of accepting an "expert opinion" of an item's value for a bona fide appraisal.

Start your search by checking with fellow collectors, dealers, and auction houses, and these accepted appraisal groups:

- **The American Society of Appraisers:** www.appraisers.org; (800) ASA-VALU; (703) 478-2228.
- **The Appraisers Association of America:** www.appraisersassoc.org; (212) 889-5404.
- **The International Society of Appraisers:** www.isa-appraisers.org; (888) 472-5587.

Should I Carry Separate Insurance on My Collection?
Maybe yes, maybe no. You need to weigh the cost of the insurance against the value of your collection and the financial impact of losing it. Some regular homeowner's policies may cover your collection. Others may require a special rider or even a completely separate policy. For insurance purposes, Mid-Century Modern collectibles usually are treated as art or antiques and so probably fall into the latter category. In the end, it all depends on the total value of your collection, what specific types of items you collect and their individual value, the terms of your current household-goods and/or homeowner's policy, and your insurance company.

Start by having a frank discussion with your insurance agent about the actual coverage your collection would have in the event of theft or fire, earthquake, or water damage. If the coverage isn't sufficient, the agent should be able to give you various options for adequate coverage in case of a loss. Many policies exclude coverage from certain types of losses, such as those caused by floods and earthquakes, so be sure to ask about any exclusions. Also find out how your policy provides for covering the increased value of your collection due to price appreciation, which, if you're lucky, may outstrip the indexed inflation rates to which replacement values may be pegged by your insurer.

Appraising the Appraisers

Try to interview several appraisers before deciding on the one person you'll entrust with valuing your prized collection. Be sure to ask:

- **What is your specific experience with Mid-Century Modern?** Ask to see resources and materials to back up their answer, such as documentation of similar appraisals.
- **Have you written articles or books, and on what subjects?**
- **Have you had professional training or taken specific courses of study, or is your experience entirely field-based?**
- **How will you determine your fee?** Be wary of any appraiser who bases the fee on the value of your item or collection. Most will charge you an hourly rate plus any expenses incurred in researching information specific to your collection.

George Nelson table clock for Howard Miller, 15" l x 3" w x 6" h. Complete with barometer and thermometer, this clock is covered in hand-stitched leather. *Photo courtesy of Wright.*

LIVING WITH YOUR COLLECTION

Collections are meant to be enjoyed. And displaying a collection is one of the true joys of this pursuit. It gives the collector a chance to share his or her passion and explain it to others.

But don't mistakenly assume that your "display" needs to be some roped-off museumlike tableau or behind-closed-doors showcase. As you're about to see, most collectors of Mid-Century Modern don't just admire the items they collect—they use them, too.

Displaying Your Collection

What's the Best Way to Display My Pieces?

Most Mid-Century collectibles tend to be furniture pieces, lighting items, or accessory items, so it's only logical to display them in room settings. If you collect small pieces, such as studio pottery, shelves and display cases will let you display them en masse for greatest impact.

opposite page: Arne Jacobsen Oxford desk chair for Fritz Hansen. 24" l x 19" w x 48" h. The high back makes this a dynamic, imposing piece of office furniture. *Photo courtesy of Wright.*

Protecting and Storing Your Collection

What Can I Do to Protect My Collection from
Extremes of Temperature and Humidity, Mold,
Mildew, Dust, Grease, and Other Pollutants?

First, use good common sense. Every collectible has its particular set of enemies. Find out what they are for the specific items you collect. For example, furniture's enemies include direct sunlight, moisture, and humidity. Use blinds that offer some degree of protection from ultraviolet light, always use coasters on tables, and consider getting a humidifier or dehumidifier to maintain appropriate humidity levels.

And smokers take note. Tobacco smoke can build up layers of discoloring nicotine on your pieces. Unless you enjoy regularly cleaning off this buildup, consider investing in an air cleaner.

A Day in the Life . . .

Here's how one collector described the way he and his family live with their Mid-Century pieces.

"Our collection is a living collection. By that I mean we actually live with and enjoy our collection as part of our day-to-day environment. Our decor, while not strictly limited to Mid-Century Modern, is very functional and simple. We sit at a Noguchi dining table on Jens Risom chairs. We eat off Russel Wright china and use Arne Jacobsen flatware. We relax on a George Nelson daybed and put our feet up on an Eames coffee table. We actually rock in our Eames rocker. Although some care must be taken not to abuse these wonderful pieces, we use them in the way they were intended . . . enjoying them fully."

Are There Areas or Rooms of My House Where
I Shouldn't Store or Display My Collection?

Yes, and they're all the usual suspects. For storage, avoid garages, attics, and basements—areas where temperature and humidity fluctuations can wreak havoc on wood veneers and metal finishes. And think twice before setting up a display of your pieces in an area prone to excessive moisture (don't display vintage radios with chromed parts in a bathroom, for example) or airborne grease (such as near the kitchen).

What If I Collect Too Many Pieces to Display or Store at Home?

In that case, join the club—you're a bona fide collector!

It's true—many collectors of Mid-Century Modern outgrow the display and storage space available at home. If that happens to you and there are pieces you can't bring yourself to sell, consider renting off-site storage space. Look for an indoor facility that has controlled temperature and humidity. The best ones will provide dollies and hand trucks to help you transport items from your vehicle, but you'll usually have to supply your own lock or locks. A security guard should be present around the clock to ensure the safety of your items.

Take the time to carefully pack your pieces for storage. Wrap fragile items in newsprint and then bubble wrap. Place them in corrugated cardboard boxes with similarly wrapped items. And take care not to put heavy items on top of or next to lightweight fragile pieces. Wrap larger fragile pieces and furniture in blankets (which you can buy inexpensively at thrift stores). Add extra layers to items that will have other lighter pieces stacked on top of them.

Showing Your Pieces in Their Best Light

Lighting your collection is a bit of a balancing act. You want to display it at its best yet protect it from the potentially damaging effects of sunlight and some artificial lighting. Direct sun can fade paint finishes and dry out wood and wood veneers in a surprisingly short time; treat your wood furniture to an application of the appropriate wax several times a year to protect it.

Also be cautious about lighting plastic items, which can break down under continuous exposure to fluorescent lighting. And although they put out a lot of light, halogen lights also give off a tremendous amount of heat. Keep your collection a safe distance away from them, and don't use halogen lights for paper goods without the appropriate filters. Consult a lighting professional to determine which fixtures are appropriate for your specific needs.

> ### *Out of Sight Shouldn't Be Out of Mind*
> Please . . . don't make the mistake of storing items and then forgetting about them. Check the pieces at your storage facility at least two or three times a year to make sure they're safe, secure, and undamaged. Pay special attention to any strong odors—they can be a sign that moisture damage has occurred even if there are no current signs of it.

How Concerned Should I Be About the Security of My Collection?

It all depends on how you'd like to live with it. In some instances, you may feel uncomfortable leaving an item of extreme value on display. Of course, the item should be insured, but the decision of how to display it is a personal one. If you're comfortable displaying the item and you enjoy having it accessible on a day-to-day basis, then for you it's probably worth any risk of its being damaged or stolen. On the other hand, if you feel anxious about displaying the object, you may want to keep it in a locked cabinet or safe. If that's not possible—as with large furniture pieces, for example—an alarm system may be the best compromise.

Caring For and Cleaning Your Collection

Are There Any Special Dos and Don'ts for Cleaning My Pieces?

Are there ever! First, realize that many collectors often inadvertently harm their pieces by overcleaning them. Use a light touch and only the appropriate cleaning agents. Or . . . use none at all: The fading of color and the buildup of light soil are natural to the aging process and can add to the patina of a piece. Some collectors insist that a great "untouched" surface is better than one that's been fastidiously overcleaned.

- If you collect dinnerware—and even if you use it every day—never put it in the dishwasher. Dishwasher detergents contain abrasives that, over time, will wear away the decals on your dinnerware or score the pieces, leaving small scratchlike marks. Of course, by hand-washing, you run a greater risk of breaking a piece. But hand-washing is more likely to guarantee a longer life for your collectibles.

- On plastics, including Lucite and Plexiglas, never use aerosol sprays or waxes. They can "fog" the plastic and permanently alter its appearance.

- Furniture pieces are best cleaned with a very mild soap-and-water mixture. This may be the only cleaning necessary. Some collectors prefer Murphy's Oil Soap for regular cleaning and a high-quality lemon oil to replenish moisture. To remove water marks or rings, try a very light rubbing with cigarette ashes, which act as a mild abrasive.

- To remove the residue from price stickers or other applied labels without damaging the wood surface, use a specialized cleaning product such as Goo Gone.

Making Minor Repairs

I Have a Few Pieces that Need Small Repairs.
Should I Try to Make Them Myself?

Maybe yes and maybe no. You need to keep in mind that any repair has the potential to harm the value of a piece; a poor repair can be worse than the original flaw. On the other hand, lightly touching up a piece of furniture or rewiring a nonworking lamp may increase the piece's value—or at least improve its chances of selling—because it makes the item more attractive or useful.

If you have a special interest in making small repairs yourself, learn what's involved from a professional first. And if you're at all unsure of your abilities, by all means leave repairs to professionals. The potential loss of value to your prized piece far outweighs the relatively small expense of a professional repair.

One last word: Whenever you sell an item that you've repaired or had repaired by professionals, it's only fair to inform the potential buyer about the alterations.

Do You Mean that Even a Small Repair
I Make Myself Could Hurt the Value of My Piece?

Yes—that's *exactly* what we mean. It all depends on the quality of the repair, how minor it really is, and, of course, the value of the piece itself. Without the proper training, you'd be wise to undertake very little repair work yourself. A damaged piece left in as-is condition may be worth more than one that's been inexpertly repaired.

"How Mid-Century Modern Changed My Life"

Most people begin to collect Mid-Century Modern as a hobby. For a lucky few, however, their passion also becomes their profession. One collector turned his love of Mid-Century Modern into a new Internet career.

Several years ago, he innocently started his own Web site—simply as an expedient means of selling a few pieces from his burgeoning collection. "The Web site began as a part-time business just to sell some of the items that I had accumulated over years of collecting. I had sold some items at a few different dealer cooperatives, but the Web site provided a more time-efficient way to accomplish the same goal. As the site developed, I began to design Web sites for other Mid-Century Modern dealers and linked to them from my site. Now my site basically serves as a gateway to many of the better Modern Web sites on the Internet. I quit my full-time job of 14 years as a pharmacist to devote my full attention to my Web site. I guess what began as a collection ultimately altered the way I live my life on a daily basis."

Undertaking Major Repairs and Restorations of Mid-Century Pieces

What If a Piece I Own or Want to Buy Needs Major Repairs?

Then it's time to really do your homework. Call on your network of fellow collectors and dealers to advise you. They likely will be able to give you the names of people who can repair your particular piece.

The importance of having quality repairs done by a qualified professional can't be overstated. Improving the visual appearance of a collectible usually will enhance its value. But repairs that detract from a piece's appearance—or that significantly alter its construction—most likely will reduce its value.

But what if you're considering the purchase of a piece that needs extensive repair. Keep in mind that repainting, rechroming, and refinishing can be expensive. And even though they'll enhance the appearance of a piece, the end result rarely will be worth as much as a piece that's still in original condition. A good rule of thumb is to try to pay no more than 50 percent of what an original-condition piece is worth. If you pay much more, in the end you may invest more in the piece than you'd pay for an example that's still in good condition. It's also important to locate a qualified repair person before you make your purchase.

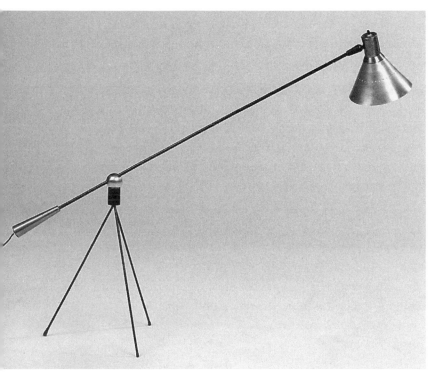

Gilbert Watrous floor lamp for Heifetz. In 1951, this lamp won the Museum of Modern Art's Low Cost Lighting Competition. *Photo courtesy of Wright.*

I Have a Piece I'd Like to Repair, Even Though I Know It Might Not Be Worth the Cost. What Should I Do?

A piece that has sentimental value can provide satisfaction well beyond its monetary worth. If repairing such an item makes it more enjoyable—or simply useful—by all means, consider it. This route is also an option for pieces that are in poor condition but that you'd still like to add to your collection until a better example comes along.

A word of caution: If the piece has historical importance, think twice about repairing it. Remember that you have a responsibility to the future. Take good care of the item while you own it. Don't change the original finish to suit your idea of fashion. Preserve the item for the future. It's the right thing to do.

"Trendy" Refinishing

There's refinishing . . . and then there's refinishing. Some dealers in large metropolitan areas specialize in nothing but refinished items, and although many of their new finishes are better than the originals, they may be different—or updated to match current decorating trends.

Not that there's anything wrong with that. But serious collectors view these pieces as fashion furniture, not true collectibles. The "new" finish might add temporary appeal, but it won't add to the piece's long-term value as a collectible. For example, many fine antiques were stripped to golden oak or painted white in the 1970s. At the time they looked great, but their long-term value was compromised.

Are There Any Safety Concerns I Should Be Aware of with Mid-Century Collectibles?

Not really. Some pottery pieces from the period used lead-base glazes, so it would be wise to use only dishes that specifically were designed as dinnerware at the table. Also, some Italian ceramics were designed as decorative pieces only and shouldn't be used for food or beverage service.

IF AND WHEN YOU DECIDE TO SELL

Why You Might Want to Sell Pieces from Your Collection

There are as many reasons to sell pieces from your collection as there are collectors themselves. Perhaps you'd like to trade up from a so-so example to a truly outstanding one. Maybe you've accumulated a number of duplicate pieces that you'd like to winnow down. Perhaps your interest in Mid-Century Modern has waned (incredible as that may be to believe), and you'd like to explore another field of collecting. Or maybe you just need the money.

You Want to Trade Up to Better Examples

Collections are dynamic. Over time, they not only increase in scope and size, but they also change in focus. You may grow tired of a particular collectible that you were quite fond of last year. A beginning collector usually starts out on a small scale, both in terms of quantity and price. But a more experienced collector has higher expectations about the quality of the items he or she buys. As you become more confident, you'll no doubt want to trade up to more desirable and usually more expensive items.

You've Acquired Duplicate Pieces You No Longer Need
As you become more knowledgeable and confident as a collector, you may notice underpriced items that aren't particularly appealing to you personally. And you may purchase them just because they're a bargain and you might be able to make a profit by reselling them. You can quickly accumulate quite an inventory of these items, which you probably won't want to keep as part of your permanent collection.

Where to Sell

Local Dealers

An obvious choice is to take your cache to a dealer who specializes in Mid-Century Modern—perhaps one where you regularly shop. But realize that most Mid-Century dealers rely on an average 100 percent markup. This means that if you'd normally see the item priced at $100 in their shop, they're not likely to pay you more than $50 for it. Is this fair? Certainly, the dealer has expenses to meet, many of which may not be obvious to the casual shopper. In addition to the cost of renting space in which to do business, the dealer has utility expenses, advertising expenses, travel expenses, and possibly payroll expenses. And last but not least, the dealer wants to be able to take home enough to pay his or her own salary.

Is this the best place to sell your pieces? Perhaps—if you regularly expect to pick up and sell items and your main goal is to turn a quick, though likely modest, profit on them. You also may build a tremendous amount of goodwill in the process: The shop owner may cut you better price breaks on items you purchase because of your regular business.

Consignment Selling

If your goal is to maximize your profit, consignment selling may be a better alternative—especially if you're intent on selling locally and you have a good rapport with a specific dealer. Many shops will sell your items in their stores for a commission on the final selling price. They benefit by not having to pay up front for the item; you benefit because you may receive a higher selling price. Of course, if the item never sells, you receive nothing. And in some cases, you may wait for several weeks or months for the item to sell.

Auctions

Another alternative is to place your items in an auction, either locally or on the Internet. If the items are highly collectible, you may do fine selling them through a local auction house, even though they may not always sell at the prices you seek.

That's why many collectors and dealers have turned to online auctions as a means of quickly and successfully selling their pieces. You reach a much larger audience to bid on your items, the auctions usually are over in 7 to 10 days, and you can set reserve prices below which you won't sell. Another benefit is that buyers sometimes get caught up in bidding wars that drive your items to final selling prices far in excess of their market value.

Advertisements

You can also sell your items through ads in local newspapers and trade publications or in the classified sections of Web sites. Newspapers tend to have the highest rates and so may not be cost-effective for less expensive items. And the market in your particular area might not be strong for the specific item you want to sell.

Trade publications usually have lower ad rates, and the audience you reach is more targeted and broad-based. This usually gives you greater leverage as a seller. Web sites may be better still; they reach a broad but targeted audience, and the cost of advertising on them is usually minimal or nonexistent.

Antiques Malls and Cooperatives

If you have a lot of items to sell, antiques malls and cooperatives can help. They'll rent you a booth or space where you can set up your own "shop." Some cooperatives may require you to work a certain number of days per month as part of your agreement; this helps reduce their overhead and protect their profit margin. In a few areas of the country, there even are 20th-century-specific cooperatives. Still another benefit: You'll likely run across opportunities to buy pieces for your own collection or to resell. But one drawback is the amount of time involved in keeping merchandise stocked, cleaned, and rotated—not to mention the possible work requirements. If the latter are a problem, you may be able to negotiate a higher monthly rent in lieu of the work requirements.

Timo Saarpeneva Orchid vase for Iittala. In 1954, this 10½" high vase was voted Most Beautifully Designed Object of the Year by *House Beautiful. Photo courtesy of Wright.*

Online Selling

Today, many Mid-Century collectors (and dealers) are establishing their own Web sites. At these online "shops," pieces are available to a worldwide audience 24 hours a day, seven days a week.

Describing Your Items for Sale

First of all, remember that the more information you provide, the better. At the very least, list the designer, the manufacturer, the pattern, the condition, and of course the price. Then mention ways buyers might use or display the item or factors that make it especially desirable. Also describe any repairs or difficult-to-find flaws in the item. In the long run, you'll reap more by forging a reputation as an honest seller than you'd ever gain by failing to disclose pertinent information about an item.

Franco Albini
lounge chairs for
Poggi Milan, 1959.
*Photo courtesy
of Wright.*

Selling Online

Online auctions are perhaps the best way for new collectors of Mid-Century Modern to sell their pieces. But you need to remember that most online auctions rely on their internal search engines to steer prospective bidders to items. For example, if a bidder happens to be looking for Franciscan Starburst china, you as the seller would be remiss to leave out the manufacturer's name (Franciscan) or the pattern name (Starburst), because those are the most likely words potential buyers will search for.

Here are examples of online auction descriptions:

A Poorly Written Description

Title: Starburst Teapot with Lid

Description: This teapot has a unique design that goes well with '50s decor.

A Well-Written Description

Title: Franciscan (Fransiscan) Starburst Teapot with Lid

Description: This wonderful Franciscan Teapot is in the highly desirable Starburst pattern. The rarely found lid also is present, and both are in mint condition. The teapot measures 8" wide and 6" high. Shipping/insurance within the continental U.S. will add $8 to the winning bid.

Key words: collectible dinnerware, '50s china, atomic, Mid-Century Modern, Eames, Russel Wright

Notice that the second description also includes a misspelled version of the manufacturer's name. By including the misspelled name, you ensure that you also get the attention of collectors who may enter a more phonetic spelling.

The last line includes key words that will also bring up this specific item in searches. This is a common way to gain more attention for your item. If you do a search for the key word "Eames" on most online auctions, you may get hundreds of results with only a few of them actually auctioning off Eames items. Many online sellers will work the key words into the item description rather than list them separately. That may not be the best idea; in the actual item description, try to use only terms that are relevant to the item you're selling.

Donating Your Collection

If you ever decide to donate your collection, you may be able to take a tax deduction—depending on how you file and the organization to whom you're donating. You must itemize in order to obtain this deduction, and the organization generally must be a qualified charitable, nonprofit, or governmental agency. To find out whether a specific organization qualifies, contact it directly.

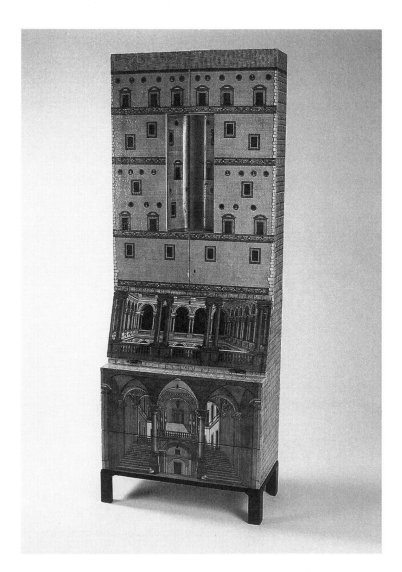

Piero Fornasetti Architettura cabinet; hand painted and lithographically printed wood, metal, and glass; 32" l x 16" w x 86" h; c. 1958. Modified from a Gio Ponti–designed form, Architettura is one of Fornasetti's finest pieces. This early example is one of about 20 produced in the 1950s and '60s. *Photo courtesy of Wright.*

Legal Obligations When You Sell

Every state and locality has its own rules governing the collection of taxes and the operation of businesses. Even if you're buying and selling as part of a hobby, you still may have legal obligations that may not be immediately obvious. For example, you may be required to obtain licenses or to collect and pay sales taxes. Check with your accountant or local Department of Taxation for the specific requirements that may apply to you.

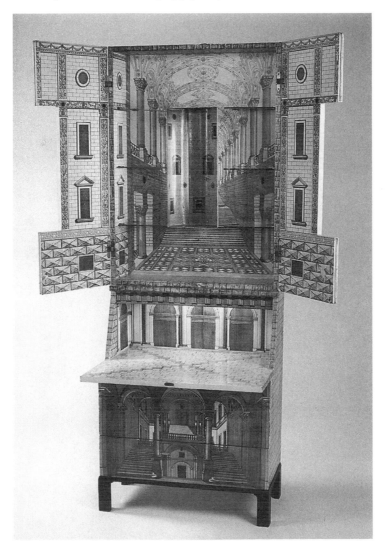

Arne Jacobsen teak dining chairs for Fritz Hansen, 1955.
Photo courtesy of Wright.

Shows

Art Deco-50s Show
Concourse Exhibition Center
635 8th Ave., San Francisco, CA 94118
Telephone: (415) 490-5800
Presented by Peter and Deborah Keretsztury
Telephone: (415) 599-3326
Web site: www.deco-echoes.com/deco50/spot.html
Comments: This West Coast show is held each year in June and
    December.

Manhattan Antiques & Collectibles
Triple Pier Expo
Piers 88, 90, and 92, West 48th to 55th Streets and 12th Avenue in
    Manhattan
Presented by Stella Show Management
147 West 24th Street
New York, NY 10011
Telephone: (212) 255-0020
Fax: (212) 255-0002
E-mail: jstella327@aol.com
Web site: www.stellashows.com
Comments: You'll see items you've seen only in books and museums
    at this show. There are three different piers, but Pier 88 is the one
    that concentrates on Mid-Century and other Modern design

movements. Don't discount the other piers, however; many times they'll yield items of interest. Usually takes place in March and November on adjacent weekends, with the first weekend getting the biggest buzz.

Miami Modernism Show
Radisson Deauville Resort
6701 Collins Avenue
Miami, FL 33141
Presented by Caussin Productions
43½ N. Saginaw
Pontiac, MI 48342
Telephone: (248) 334-9660
Fax: (248) 253-1883
E-mail: jcaussin@aol.com
Web site: www.machineage.com/miami/
Comments: This show usually features the finest dealers and takes place the same week as some other major 20th-century shows, such as the Art Deco Weekend and various flea markets.

Michigan Modernism Exposition
Southfield Civic Center
26000 Evergreen
Southfield, MI 48037
Presented by M&M Enterprises
19946 Great Oaks Circle South
Clinton Township, MI 48036-4401
Phone: (810) 469-1706 or (810) 465-9441
Fax: (810) 468-5694
E-mail: mandminfo@aol.com
Web site: www.deco-echoes.com/expo/index.html
Comments: A very good show that takes place each spring.

Specialist Dealers

Note: For these shops, always call ahead to verify hours of operation. Many of them are small and may be closed when their owners attend shows.

Form and Function
95 Vandam Street
New York, NY 10013
Telephone: (212) 414-1800
Web site: www.formandfunctiondesign.com
Comments: A relatively new store and Web site that showcases some excellent examples.

Good Eye 20th-Century Interiors
4918 Wisconsin Avenue NW
Washington, D.C. 20016
Telephone: (202) 244-8516
Fax: (202) 244-8517

Web site: www.goodeyeonline.com

Comments: This shop features interesting displays and showcases the owner's interior-design expertise. Located just north of the Georgetown area in a quaint neighborhood.

Lumiere

112 N. Third Street

Philadelphia, PA 19106

Telephone: (215) 922-6908

Web site: www.gomod.com/mall/lumiere/home.htm

Comments: This smaller shop has been in business for several years just a block south of Mode Moderne. Some great finds can be had here, and the selection usually is quite interesting, with a mixture of high design and unusual anonymous pieces.

Millennium

1528 U Street N.W.

Washington, D.C. 20009

Telephone: (202) 483-1218

Web site: www.millenniumdc.com

Comments: A few years ago, there were quite a few shops that featured Mid-Century designs in the D.C. area. Now there are basically three. This one is a cooperative that features many different dealers in one shop. An eclectic mix can be found here, and the shop caters to an equally eclectic clientele. You're as likely to find a new college graduate just decorating his first apartment as a longtime collector perusing the wares. Merchandise changes often, and stories are legendary about the great finds that have come out of this row-house shop. Some interesting restaurants are close by, so don't miss this shop when you're in the D.C. area.

Mint

91 Wall Street

Seattle, WA 98111

Telephone: 206-956-8270

Fax: 206-443-0350

E-mail: mint@drizzle.com

Comments: This shop sells Mid-Century Modern office furniture.

Standard Home

1108 Pike Street

Seattle, WA 98101

Telephone: 206-464-0850

Comments: In this shop you'll find Mid-Century furniture for the home.

Mode Moderne

159 North Third Street

Philadelphia, PA 19106

Telephone: (215) 627-0299

Fax: (215) 627-1499

Web site: www.modemoderne.com

Comments: This was one of the first shops in the country to sell Modern designs exclusively, and it's still going strong. You'll also find Mode Moderne at many of the major shows around the country.

The ModHaus

Telephone: (617) 464-4485

Web site: www.modhaus.com

Comments: Although currently exclusively on the Internet, this virtual shop has cultivated a loyal following, including many dealers. It seems to find wonderful items and often offers them at surprisingly low prices.

1950

Telephone: (404) 577-9271

Web site: www.1950.com

Comments: This site features a wide array of Mid-Century Modern merchandise.

Auction Houses and Auctions

David Rago Auctions

333 North Main Street

Lambertville, NJ 08530

Telephone: (609) 397-9374

Fax: (609) 397-9377

Web site: www.ragoarts.com

Comments: Features both Arts and Crafts auctions and 20th-Century auctions, many times one following the other. Prospective bidders usually can preview items the week before the auction.

Los Angeles Modern Auctions

P.O. Box 462006

Los Angeles, CA 90046

Telephone: (323) 904-1950

Fax: (323) 904-1954

E-mail: peter@lamodern.com

Web site: www.lamodern.com

John Toomey Gallery

818 North Boulevard

Oak Park, IL 60301

Telephone: (708) 383-5234

Fax: (708) 383-4828

E-mail: toomey@interaccess.com

Web site: www.treadwaygallery.com

Treadway Gallery Incorporated

2029 Madison Road

Cincinnati, OH 45208

Telephone: (513) 321-6742

Fax: (513) 871-7722

E-mail: treadway2029@earthlink.net

Web site: www.treadwaygallery.com

Comments: Both the John Toomey Gallery and Treadway Gallery Incorporated have

Arts and Crafts auctions and 20th-century auctions. Their catalogs and publications are always in demand as references on the pricing of specific items.

Wright
1140 W. Fulton
Chicago, IL 60607
Telephone: (312) 563-0020
Comments: A gallery and boutique auction house specializing in Mid-Century design.

Trade Papers and Magazines

Antique Trader Weekly
100 Bryant Street
P.O. Box 1050
Dubuque, IA 52004-1050
Telephone: (800) 334-7165
Fax: (800) 531-0880
Web site: www.collect.com/antiquetrader
Comments: An extensive listing of pottery, art glass, and china for sale in a classified-ad format. This publication also features informational articles and advertisements of upcoming auctions throughout the country; it's more focused on general antiques.

***Echoes* Magazine**
P.O. Box 155
Cummaquid, MA 02637
Telephone: (508) 362-3822
Fax: (508) 362-6670
Web site: www.deco-echoes.com
Comments: Features information on shops and shows, a calendar of events, and articles on a variety of topics. It's a good resource for shop locations as well.

***Metropolis* Magazine**
P.O. Box 609
Mt. Morris, IL 61054
Telephone: (800) 344-3046
Web site: www.metropolismag.com
Comments: This magazine caters more to interior designers, but it also features regular articles and advertisements on Mid-Century Modern.

***Metropolitan Home* Magazine**
1633 Broadway
New York, NY 10019
Telephone: (303) 604-1464
Comments: A mainstream interior-design magazine that often features homes decorated with Mid-Century furnishings. This magazine doesn't provide much in the way of information, but it shows ways to decorate with Mid-Century pieces.

Modernism **Magazine**
333 North Main Street
Lambertville, NJ 08530
Telephone: (609) 397-4104
Web site: www.ragoarts.com/nj/modsub.html
Comments: The same people who conduct the Rago Auctions produce this magazine.
Wallpaper
Brettenham House
Lancaster Place
London WC2E7TL
England
Telephone: (44) 171-322-1177
Fax: (44) 171-322-1171
E-mail: wallpaper_mag@time-inc.com
Wallpaper TNT International Express
P.O. Box 9018
Jericho, NY 11753
Telephone: (813) 348-4121

Fax: (813) 348-4073
Comments: An import magazine popular with Mid-Century collectors published nine
    times per year. Look for it at larger bookstores or specialty magazine and book
    dealers, or inquire about subscribing at the address above.

Clubs and Collecting Associations

There are so many clubs that it would be impossible to mention them all here. To see a listing of more than 900 collecting clubs, many related to Mid-Century collecting, visit Collectorsonline.com at http://www.collectoronline.com/club-directory.shtml.

Most clubs and associations are quite specific to particular interest groups. There aren't many general groups devoted to Mid-Century design.

Here's a sampling of what you'll find:

- The Art Pottery Association, American (Patti Bourgeois, contact; Jean Oberkirsch, sec.), P.O. Box 525, Cedar Hill, MO 63016.
- The Eva Zeisel Collectors Club, 22781 Flamingo St., Woodland Hills, CA 91364.
- The Glaze, Pottery Collectors' Newsletter, P.O. Box 4782, Birmingham, AL 35706.
- Homer Laughlin China Collectors Association, P.O. Box 26021, Crystal City, VA 22215-6021; e-mail: fiesta@mediumgreen.com; Web site: http://www.medium-green.com/hlcca.

Online Auctions and Marketers

Amazon.com
Probably the next-best auction site for Mid-Century items. Amazon.com joined the auction fray relatively recently and is set up similar to eBay. The site has teamed up with Sotheby's to offer a higher caliber of items and to give buyers a guarantee. And with their

LiveBid Auctions, a collector can bid on items at live auctions from their home computer. Several 20th-century auctions have already been featured.

eBay.com
Currently the most dominant online auction site; there are literally more than a million items on auction at any given time. A wide range of Mid-Century collectibles is always up for bid. Try searching with the following key words: eames, george nelson, herman miller, knoll, and danish modern. If you're looking for Mid-Century china, try looking up russel wright, zeisel, seibel, or franciscan starburst.

E-Groups

Many Web sites now offer discussion boards and list servers to facilitate the exchange of information. For example, GoMod.com is developing a separate Web site just for interaction among collectors and site visitors. This Web site, objectculture.com, will feature live and scheduled chat-room events and discussion boards relating to all areas of Mid-Century collectibles. DesignAddict.com, a Belgian Web site, currently offers two discussion boards—one devoted to identifying objects and the other devoted to general discussions on design.

There is also an e-mail discussion group for Mid-Century design located at onelist.com. Just search "midcenturymodern" to locate and sign up. You'll have the option to receive a digest of the day's e-mails, to receive the e-mails as they're sent, or to visit the site to retrieve postings.

Museums and Galleries

Cooper-Hewitt National Design Museum
Smithsonian Institution
2 East 91st Street
New York, NY 10128-0606
Telephone: (212) 849-8400

The Museum of Modern Art (MOMA)
11 West 53rd Street
New York, NY 10019
Telephone: (212) 708-9400
Web site: www.moma.org

Philadelphia Museum of Art
26th Street and the Benjamin Franklin Parkway
Philadelphia, PA 19130
Telephone: (215) 763-8100
Web site: www.philamuseum.org

Historic Sites

Eames Office Archive and Gallery
2665 Main Street, Suite E
Santa Monica, CA 90405
Telephone: (310) 396-5991

Manitoga
Home and landscape created by Russel Wright
P.O. Box 249, Route 9D
Garrison, NY 10524
Telephone: (914) 424-3812
Fax: (914) 424-4043
Web site: www.manitoga.org
Comments: Advance reservations are required.

Libraries

There's an extensive online collection to browse at the Library of Congress Web site located at: http://lcweb.loc.gov/.

The Museum of Modern Art also maintains an extensive library on art and design.

Specialists in Repair, Restoration, and Conservation

Most areas that have Mid-Century shops will have artisans who are capable of repairing Mid-Century Modern collectibles. It's best to check with shop owners in your area for the best recommendations of specific repair or restoration specialists.

Manufacturers

Herman Miller for the Home
855 East Main Avenue
Zeeland, MI 49464-0302
Telephone: 800-646-4400
Web site: www.hmhome.com

Knoll, Inc.
1235 Water Street
East Greenville, PA 18041
Telephone: 877-61-KNOLL
Web site: www.knoll.com

RECOMMENDED BOOKS

Mid-Century Modern: Furniture of the 1950s
By Cara Greenberg and Tim Street-Porter (photographer)
Harmony Books, New York
Published 1984
Comments: This book was many collectors' first exposure to Mid-Century Modern
as a field of collecting. A mixture of archival photos, interiors, and illustrations,
it provides a wealth of information on collecting Mid-Century designs. The
hard-to-find hardback version is itself now a collectible.

Contemporary: Architecture and Interiors of the 1950s
By Lesley Jackson
Phaidon Press, Inc.
Published 1994
Comments: A beautiful book that features interiors and architecture of the period.

Modern Furniture Classics Since 1945
By Charlotte Feill and Peter Feill
AIA Press
Published 1991
Comments: 192 pages full of the best in international design in modern furniture;
beautiful color photos along with black-and-white images.

The New Look: Design in the 1950s
By Lesley Jackson
Thames & Hudson
Published 1991 (hardcover), 1998 (paperback)
Comments: A survey of major categories of 1950s design—profiling prominent
designers, important companies, and their significant works—fashion, furni-
ture, lighting, glass, silver, wallpaper, and textiles

*Design 1935–1965: What Modern Was: Selections from the Liliane and David
M. Stewart Collection*
By Martin Eidelberg (editor) Le Musee des arts decoratifs de Montreal/Abrams
Published 1991
Comments: Focuses on 200 of the finest objects from the most important designers
and artists of the time. There's an essay by historian Paul Johnson on the politi-
cal background of the years 1935–1965, and each chapter opens with an
insightful examination of each style. The individual entries, by noted experts in
the fields of furniture, ceramics, glass, textiles, metalwork, and graphic design,
present a wealth of information on the works as well as an understanding of
their techniques. Detailed biographies of the designers and histories of the
companies responsible for creating the objects make this book an invaluable
reference tool.

MID-CENTURY MODERN GLOSSARY

Bauhaus: A school of thought formed in Germany that led the way to Mid-Century Modern design later in the century. Based on the "form follows function" edict, it spawned many designs that had a rather clinical and boxy appearance and used materials such as concrete and steel for their construction.

Contemporary: Generally refers to the entire lifestyle concept popularized alongside Mid-Century Modern furnishings. Many modern homes of the era that featured open spaces and flat or angled roofs are referred to as contemporary.

Danish Modern: At the same time that Mid-Century Modern was taking hold in the United States, a comparable style based more on craftsmanship and featuring solid woods more prominently was gaining popularity. This style, which is akin to Mid-Century Modern, was to achieve phenomenal success in the United States as well.

Kitsch: Refers to pieces with a derivative style that have similarities to items of good design but that usually are adorned with unnecessary elements or are of inferior quality.

Mid-Century Modern: Generally refers to a style of furnishings that was popular after World War II (1947–1957).

Post-Modern: A style made popular in the 1980s by an Italian firm known as Memphis. It featured wild laminated surfaces, bright colors, and almost comical designs that seemed to poke fun at Modern design.

20th-Century Design: Refers to any design style created or popularized during the 20th century. This can include Mid-Century Modern, Art Deco or Moderne, Post-Modern, Mission, and '60s Pop, among others.

ABOUT THE INTERNATIONAL SOCIETY OF APPRAISERS

The *Collector's Compass* series is endorsed by the International Society of Appraisers, one of North America's leading nonprofit associations of professionally educated and certified personal property appraisers. Members of the ISA include many of the industry's most respected independent appraisers, auctioneers, and dealers. ISA appraisers specialize in more than 200 areas of expertise in four main specialty pathways: antiques and residential contents, fine art, gems and jewelry, and machinery and equipment.

Established in 1979 and consisting of more than 1,375 members, the ISA is founded on two core principles: educating its members through a wide range of continuing education and training opportunities, and promoting and maintaining the highest ethical and professional standards in the field of appraisals.

Education through the ISA

In conjunction with the University of Maryland University College, the ISA offers a series of post-secondary professional courses in appraisal studies, including a two-level certification program.

The ISA recognizes three membership levels within its organization—Associate Member, Accredited Member, and Certified Member—with educational programs in place for achieving higher distinctions within the society. ISA members who complete the required course work are recognized with the title of Certified Appraiser of Personal Property (CAPP). Through its pioneering education programs, the ISA plays a vital role in producing qualified appraisers in appraisal theory, principles, procedures, ethics, and law as it pertains to personal property appraisal.

Professional Standards of the ISA

The ISA is dedicated to the highest ethical standards of conduct, ensuring public confidence in the ability and qualifications of its members. To help members perform their work with the most up-to-date knowledge of professional standards, the ISA is continually updating, expanding, and improving its courses and criteria of conduct.

For more information about the International Society of Appraisers, contact their corporate offices:

Toll-free: 1-800-472-4732
E-mail: ISAHQ@isa-appraisers.org
Web site: www.isa-appraisers.org

ABOUT THE CONTRIBUTORS

Barry Bryant has been on a continual collecting spree for the past nine years. Beginning his collection with a kitschy 1950s lime-green ballerina lamp, this one-time pharmacist was on his way toward finding a new career—although his success might have been difficult to predict at the start. While setting up a booth at an antiques show years ago, only one item sold, and thoughts of business success were dashed. Later stints in three different antiques malls were semisuccessful, but when Mr. Bryant launched his GoMod.com Web site in 1998, it began to appear that the dream of "hobby as career" finally was a possibility. Initially developed as a site to sell off collection overflow, it quickly developed into a destination site for collectors of 20th-century design. With the success of this site and the help of his longtime partner John McLendon, Mr. Bryant finally threw in the mortar and pestle after fourteen years and embarked on his dream. He can be reached through the GoMod Web site or at (877) 56-GO-MOD.

Richard Wright has been a dealer in Modern design since 1985. An internationally recognized authority in American postwar design, Mr. Wright runs a specialty auction house and gallery in Chicago. He can be contacted directly at 1140 W. Fulton, Chicago, Illinois 60607; (312) 563-0020.

Christopher J. Kuppig has spent his entire career in book publishing. For several years he directed programs at Dell Publishing, Consumer Reports Books, and most recently Chilton Book Company—where his assignments included managing the Wallace-Homestead and Warman's lines of antiques and collectibles guides.

In 1997, Mr. Kuppig founded Stone Studio Publishing Services, a general management consultancy to book publishers. Acting as Series Editor for the Collector's Compass series has given him the opportunity to draw upon his wide-ranging network of contacts in the collecting field.

Mr. Kuppig resides with his wife and three children in eastern Massachusetts.

INDEX

127